Praise for *The Akashic Records*

"Throughout the ages there have been only a few teachers who have found clear and concise ways to bring forth information that might otherwise be so entangled in mystery as to be impossible to understand. Ernesto Oritz has embraced the compendium of mystical information, often called the Book of Life, and developed a teachings that revels how to access this knowledge. He skillfully holds our attention, just as he does in his workshops, delighting us with his expertise and personal insights while making this vibrant and rich material available to everyone."

—Lorraine Meyer, founder of Anew Reiki and Healing Arts Miami

"Over the last nine years I have seen the transformation and profoundly revitalizing new beginnings folks make as a result of attending workshops with Master teacher Ernesto Ortiz. His new book *The Akashic Records* now makes many of his teachings and techniques easily assessable. I would recommend this book as an essential primer and resource guide for anyone interested in exploring the vastness of their own heart's song."

—Wendlyn A. Stauffer, owner of Villa Sumaya

"*The Akashic Records* is a beautiful manual for finding keys 'to unlocking the ineffable.' This book creates a portal for us to climb through and access all the points on the etheric map to understanding our place as spiritual beings in this human experience. He teaches us step by step to access our records and unlock our own paths to fulfillment. Ernesto brings his spirit into everything he does and this beautiful book is no exception. He has a way of transforming the mystical into an understandable and accessible form for us, untangling confusion and weaving words into clear direction to finding our way in this seemingly chaotic world. He makes us feel purposeful, both for us personally and for the whole of the world. I am honored to call Ernesto Ortiz my teacher and friend. He is a true shaman, spiritual teacher, guide and master. Ernesto's wisdom surpasses that of knowledge learned; his knowing is embedded in his soul. Ernesto is a Soul Teacher, a spirited man who walks his talk and lives his purpose. I highly recommend Ernesto's work to you as a spiritual traveler."

—Janis E. McKinstry, MA transpersonal psychology, psychospiritual counselor and consultant

D1520679

The Akashic Records

Sacred Exploration of Your Soul's Journey Within the Wisdom of the Collective Consciousness

By Ernesto Ortiz

New Page BOOKS

This edition first published in 2015 by New Page Books, an imprint of
Red Wheel/Weiser, LLC
With offices at:
65 Parker Street, Suite 7
Newburyport, MA 01950
www.redwheelweiser.com
www.newpagebooks.com

ISBN: 978-1-60163-345-3

Library of Congress Cataloging-in-Publication Data
Ortiz, Ernesto.
  The Akashic records : sacred exploration of your soul's journey within the wisdom of the collective consciousness / Ernesto Ortiz.
     pages cm
  Summary: "The Akashic Records is equal parts practical and profound, the culmination of nearly two decades of immersion by Ernesto, personally and professionally, into the Akashic Records for individual healing, growth, and self-realization"-- Provided by publisher.
  Includes bibliographical references and index.
  ISBN 978-1-60163-345-3 (paperback) -- ISBN 978-1-60163-439-9 (ebook) 1. Akashic records. I. Title.

  BF1045.A44O78 2014
  133.9--dc23
                                                          2014028053

Cover design by Howard Grossman/12E Design
Diagrams on page 48 courtesy of SSRF.
www.spiritualresearchfoundation.org.
Sacred Prayer on pages 128–129 translated by Jim Duyer: *www.event12.com.*
Interior by Gina Schenck

Printed in the United States of America
IBI
10 9 8 7 6 5 4 3 2 1

Dedication

I dedicate this book to the Masters and Teachers and the Lords of Akasha. I want to thank them for the constant inspiration and guidance they give me in my life.

Also, to each student who has shared so deeply with me in the workshops and intensives we've experienced together. This book is an outpouring of the knowledge and experience I have gained from my work with you. You all have been and continue to be an inspiration to me. Your stories and personal breakthroughs have been my primary motivations to continue teaching this material.

And finally, to my family and children, for all of their support and for putting up with me and with my crazy travel schedule.

Acknowledgments

A very special thank you to my student/friend, who did not want her name to appear in the book: Thank you for the countless hours you put into editing the manuscript—your help was invaluable.

My deepest gratitude to my friend Sushila Oliphant for the diagrams and drawings: Your help and energy throughout the years has been much appreciated.

Contents

Vision

To your tired eyes I bring a vision
of a different world,
so new and clean and fresh
you will forget the pain and sorrow
that you saw before.
Yet this is a vision
which you must share
with everyone you see,
for otherwise you will behold it not.
To give this gift is how to make it yours.

—From *A Course in Miracles* by Helen Cohn Schucman

Disclaimer

This book is intended to provide accurate and helpful information. However, readers are strongly encouraged to consult with a healthcare professional before using any of the information contained in this book. Neither the author or the publisher is engaged in rendering medical advice or services. Accordingly, the publisher and author disclaim any liability, loss, damage, or injury caused by the use or application of the contents of this work. NO WARRANTY, EXPRESS OR IMPLIED, IS DELIVERED BY THE AUTHOR OR PUBLISHER WITH RESPECT TO THE CONTENTS OF THIS WORK.

Preface:
A Unique Turning Point

As I complete this book in early 2014, quite a number of crises are putting the world on high alert. We have witnessed economic breakdowns, climate disruptions, earthquakes, tsunamis, floods, tornados, power-plant meltdowns, and more. We have seen the disruption created by oil companies and how that has affected our oceans as well as the human condition.

We see desperation and violent conflicts around the world, wars and the proliferation of weapons. We see a tremendous amount of wealth alongside desperate poverty in many countries. The world seems to be on high alert, and all of this is affecting people at a deep level. We see it when people "snap" and go on killing rampages out of a deep disconnect from themselves and from humanity. We are losing kindness and compassion. Our modern-day prophets, the movie-makers, are putting images in movies and video games that only seem to cultivate the violence and horror that are being received by the minds of our youth.

In September 2005 there was a world symposium held at Columbia University, where scientists, engineers, religious and spiritual leaders, philosophers, and economists from all over the world got together to ask one question: *What is going on with the planet?* The results were stunning. *Scientific America* published a special edition to bring the results of the symposium to people all around the globe. The title of the special edition was *Crossroads for the Planet Earth,* and the subtitle was *The Human Race Is at a Unique Turning Point.* At the end of the symposium the scientists asked us, the people of world, a question in turn: *Will we choose to create the best of all possible worlds?*

So today, in 2014, I ask myself and you, dear reader, the same question: What is going on with the planet? What is your contribution to the whole? What we have to realize is that we are both a part of the crisis *and* determiners of the outcome; our actions, at a personal level as well as a planetary level, can be part of the solution. If we do nothing, however, disaster could be the final outcome.

On top of all of this, we have ended a cosmic cycle, as prophesized by the Mayas, and are now at the beginning of another; we are entering the Age of Awakening. The Mayan prophecy that we all know about is based on the Mayan calendar, and it tells us that this cosmic cycle ended on December 21, 2012. This date also marked the end of a bigger cycle that started 5,125 years ago. This event happens every 25,920 years, the precise amount of time required for the equinox to move through all the signs of the zodiac.

The Mayan calendar doesn't talk about the end of the world; it simply talks about the end of a cycle and the beginning of a new one. Many people use the term *apocalypse* to describe this event, making a reference to the common notion of apocalypse as wholesale destruction and the end of the world. The real meaning of the term *apocalypse,* however, is not "destruction" but "lifting of the veil" or "revelation." It is my hope that this book will bring awareness to the world community, because with that awareness, the veil will be lifted, and we will have the inner revelation as to what is really going on, both microcosmically and macrocosmically.

So as I continue to explore this question, I feel as though we are passing through the thin part of a funnel, almost as though we are being squeezed. If we look back into history, at the progression of cycles of time, we'll realize it's all about the earth and the solar system moving together as a family on a journey. We are here at the end of times. We should ask ourselves: What is our personal role and contribution toward the whole, and how we can come together as a family to effect positive change in the world?

We were born knowing how to speak the language of the heart, the language of emotions; let's put those emotions in action. We must allow our hearts to remain open, free from fears and limitations, and open to listening to the wisdom of the heart and communicating with the world using the language of love, kindness, compassion, tolerance, and acceptance.

Many of the people I meet through my teachings are questioning what it means to *be here now*. Many people want to discover (or rediscover) and cultivate their spirituality. The Baby Boomers are coming back to their center, and many young people are questioning the meaning of life that has been created for them. They see that there are no real answers, so they are gravitating toward discovering their true nature, their spiritual nature. In the midst of great chaos and suffering, there is a worldwide spiritual awakening going on, and it is beautiful to witness.

As people take to a spiritual path and spiritual teachings, they realize that there is much to be healed and much to discover about the self. Many people have turned to the Akashic Records as the means to self-discovery, to heal and to receive the answers to their questions. In essence, people want to know what it means to be happy and content. They want to know how to contribute to this beautiful planet that is suffering and what they can do to heal it. We all have seeds inside of us, the seeds of human potential, kindness, tolerance, compassion, and love. These seeds enable us to put aside our differences and come together during times of disaster and suffering. When we do this, we are nourishing the seeds within, watering and feeding them so that they germinate and blossom. In this way, our connections with others deepen in love and compassion. Awakening to our spiritual nature, brought about by our yearning to find deeper meaning in our lives, also causes those seeds to germinate.

When I teach, many of my students want me to convey to them some deep and profound truth, an esoteric secret that comes from the archives of the Akashic Records. All I tell them is to continue developing the energy of love and the goodness that is within all of our hearts. Our essence is pure, and our goodness is our real nature. Let's continue focusing on the beautiful things that are happening. Let's continue focusing on the spiritual awakening that is taking place all over the world, and the way we are coming together as a global community to help those countries that have been affected by natural disasters. Let's put our attention to the levels of love and compassion that we show as a world community in times of need. The spiritual revolution that I see as I travel and teach around the world is awe-inspiring to observe. The world community is hungry for more understanding; in many ways we are returning to basics, and one of these basics is our spiritual life.

If we come together as light workers, as millions of people who care, and if we unite our hearts and minds, we can have a powerful impact on the planet, even to the point of averting potential negative outcomes. We can shift the consciousness of chaos to the consciousness of harmony and peace, as long as we learn and speak the language of the heart.

As of this writing we are at the beginning, the cusp, of another 5,125-year cycle. Whether we realize it or not, we are currently creating the foundation for yet another cosmic cycle, and our thoughts and actions will determine the quality of this new beginning. If that is not exciting, I don't know what is! Time is marching on, and all of the players are in place; it is as if the planet is poised and waiting for our contribution.

Let's remember that *we are the ones that we have been waiting for.* We are the children, we are the elders, we are the past, we are the future, we are the mystics and the shamans, we are the priests and priestesses, and we are the ancestors who carry the wisdom and the knowledge of the past with us as we shape the future.

Join me on this continued journey, the journey of the heart.

Introduction

Every book begins with a single paragraph, and this one is no different, except that this book also begins with a single, conscious breath. Pause for a moment and take a deep breath. Let it out slowly. Take a second breath, making it deep, gentle, kind, and loving, and drawing it down through your entire body. As you exhale, bring your attention to your heart. Make a commitment to yourself that every time you pick up this book, you will consciously breathe. Set the intention that you will focus your attention on your heart as you read. If you do this, you will experience the greatest possible understanding by allowing your heart to receive the information and then pass it along to your mind. I invite you to enter a space of exploration that will take you deep within yourself. I invite you to enter a space of open possibilities as we come together to understand the Akashic Records.

The journey begins with a single breath and an open heart.

We are here for a purpose that is both individual and collective. We are not here to grow; growth is inevitable—plants grow, animals grow, fish grow. However, we humans have a unique opportunity to reinvent our world and ourselves. In presenting this information, it is my deepest hope that we can all contribute to the great collective changes that are needed in the world. At the same time, most of us recognize that external change springs from individual, internal change. The information presented here can take you on a journey of self-discovery. It will give you the tools to become an architect of your own life as well as an inner archeologist. You are ready to begin the journey of uncovering and reinventing. Know that you will encounter many challenges, but recognize that they are worth the ultimate goal.

What is the ultimate goal? For many of us, the goal is the same as it has been for eons, to truly "know thyself." The goal is to know who you really are and what you are here to do, and to figure out the patterns of self-limitation that keep you from fully realizing your inner beauty, magnificence, and awakening.

As the opening question in my Akashic Records workshops, I often ask, "What makes you beautiful, talented, gorgeous, and magnificent?" In most cases, the moment the question is asked, people start shrinking, wiggling in their seats, turning red, and feeling very uncomfortable. In most cases, the response is dead silence, so I tell them I will start pointing my finger and they will all have to share. As people begin sharing, they usually talk about what they do or what they like, but only a few can speak of their "inner beauty" or "magnificence." Many people end up telling me they simply don't know. Some tell me they feel they don't deserve to be beautiful because of tragic events that have taken place in their lives. Through sincere exploration of the self using the Akashic Records, you can reach the full realization of your beauty and your magnificence. At the end of the book, I will share a beautiful poem with you that will help you understand and enter this space where you can explore and eventually own your magnificence. The only requirement is to have an open heart and the courage to look deep within.

As an architect builds, he or she checks again and again throughout the process to make sure the structure is solid and level, to ensure the structure will be able to withstand whatever comes along, be it earthquakes, storms, or strong winds. In our case, these "storms" and "earthquakes" are the strong feelings and emotions that invariably come up in life. We ensure that our lives are strong and level by having a consistent spiritual practice, by learning specific techniques, such as the Akashic Records, or by meditating. We are like airplanes: never 100 percent on track but always compensating for the wind currents and making corrections to our trajectories. In this way, we reach our destination.

But it is not just about the exterior structure. The inner archeologist is the one who is willing to explore and discover what is within. He or she knows that there is more to him- or herself than what is on the surface, that there are great depths to be explored. The inner archeologist knows that the contribution that he or she has to give to the world can only come from a space of healed self-discovery.

Many of us, especially those of us living in the Western world, have created a life of comfort and ease. We work for our money, but we are not going through the bitter and endless struggle that many people around the world go through in order to have even their most basic needs met. As such, our lives are like a beautiful green hill, fertile and well-tended. Occasionally we have the misfortune of stepping in something nasty, and we get irritated because we have to clean it up. If this happens again and again, if we keep cleaning things up only to encounter another unwanted pile, if we are wise we realize that Spirit is pushing us to enter a deeper inner space. At this point, the inner archeologist wakes up and says, *Okay, I cannot continue stepping in messes anymore; I need to look deep within and find out what is triggering all of this confusion, dissatisfaction, and turmoil in my life*. Our higher self actually creates the conditions and circumstances that enable the inner archeologist to step in.

In this way, we begin the journey of self-discovery. I like to see this adventure as tilling land that is green and fertile—something tells us we must dig. As we do, we come across skeletons, the remains of old memories of past traumas. We rediscover these past events and we feel them once again. Perhaps we have worked on this particular issue before, but for whatever reason we have not gotten to a point of complete resolution, so the energetic and emotional *charges*—the residue that comes from our interactions with others—are still there, staring us in the face. Please know that you have the archeological tools to make this journey of discovery much easier. You are not alone anymore. You have the guidance, illumination, and direction of the Masters and Teachers at your disposal. You have the Lords of Akasha taking the journey with you. Because of this, you now have the tools to bring about the complete resolution of all past events and bring all current issues to a state of total and abiding peace.

Archeologists often discover that one tribe or culture conquered and built on the ruins of the previous occupants. We, too, build experiences one on top of the other; if we don't reach complete resolution for an event or circumstance, we simply move on and bury it in the depths of our psyche. Eventually, these corpses from the past start decomposing, and little by little they create a stench that affects everything in our lives. At some point, we just can't stand it anymore, and we know we need to do something about it. Fortunately, we now have the opportunity to dig with the right tools and the right help, making this journey much more effective and rewarding.

As we uncover these corpses from the past, we will also discover the treasures, the true gems. We will be able to place them back on the altar of our heart. These are the merits we have gained, not only in this life, but those accumulated from many lifetimes. We can view it as our good karma that has brought us to this place and time to be exposed to the teachings of the Akashic Records.

Here is another way to understand this process. Imagine your life as a salt-water pond. As you move through life, twigs, branches, leaves, dust, and debris fall into the pond. Some of this material you scoop out, especially if you are following a spiritual path. This debris represents your emotions, material that will slowly sink to the bottom of the pond if you do not take care of it. Sometimes, however, we go through heavy, stressful, or traumatizing events in our lives, and we are not equipped to handle them. What we end up doing is taking those emotions, putting them inside a 50-gallon steel drum, sealing the top, and throwing it into the pond. It slowly sinks into our subconscious, and we forget all about it.

After a while, if you are able to make your life pleasant and comfortable, the pond starts looking nice and clear. You take care of what falls in, but for the most part you have it pretty good, and the pond looks beautiful and unsullied. Unfortunately, life is unpredictable, and before you know it, something happens in your life, and it is as if someone stuck a giant whisk in your clear, beautiful pond and stirred it all up. All the sediment that was at the bottom of the pond is suddenly all over the place, and the pond is not so clear anymore. With all that sediment brought to the surface, you actually have a wonderful opportunity to use the Akashic Records to start examining it and healing yourself. It is almost as if the Akashic Records were providing a great net to use to start scooping this icky stuff out of your pond.

Be forewarned: What you don't scoop out will slowly start sinking back down to the bottom of the pond, and things will start looking good again—at least on the surface, at least for a while. Don't forget that 50-gallon drum that we talked about. What is stored in that drum is like toxic waste, and the water is our very life. Over time, the steel drum corrodes. Many times we chain this drum to the bottom of the pond to make sure it doesn't come to the surface, but the corrosion of the chain and the drum eventually breaks it open. Before you know it, all of that toxic waste rises to the surface, and now you really don't have any other choice but to deal with it.

If you embrace a spiritual practice, or if you use your Akashic Records, you have wonderful tools to deal with this toxic stuff. If not, you could be at risk for a mental breakdown. Perhaps some of you have already have one, or worse. We have seen this dynamic play out in the lives of certain televangelists who preach at the masses all day long and then get caught coming out of a motel with a prostitute. Once they are exposed, instead of owning their actions, we may hear them say, "It wasn't me! The devil made me do it!" What kind of an excuse is that? Unfortunately, by not owning what has happened, and instead entering into deep denial, they court a mental breakdown. They end up taking all kinds of medications to numb themselves instead of facing the issue and exploring it to get to the root cause and heal it.

Hopefully nothing like this will never happen in your life, but if it does, you will have the tools to deal with it in the space of the most pure love of all, the space of Akasha. In this space, you will never feel or hear any words of judgment or criticism. It is a space where you will be able to go to deal safely and lovingly with all the material that has accumulated in your pond.

Are you ready to start exploring? Let's go!

1

What Are the Akashic Records?

The word *Akasha* is a Sanskrit word that means, variously, "primordial substance," "ether," "sky" or "cosmos." The Akashic Records hold the records of all circumstances and actions concerning consciousness in all realities. They hold the story of your soul's evolution from its inception up until the present time. They are the sum of all knowledge, past and present, and they contain the possibility of the unfolding of all future events (based on the choices that we make). The Akashic Records are essentially a compendium of all knowledge of the human experience encoded and stored in a non-physical (i.e., spiritual) plane of existence called *Akasha*. I like to think of them as the Library of Congress of the soul. They are the recordings of your progression of lives, inscribed in your own personal Book of Life.

Every experience, thought, and emotion of every living thing, human and animal, is kept in this cosmic library. Every life form both contributes to and has access to the Records. Some philosophers, psychics, mystics, and spiritual practitioners believe that the events recorded upon Akasha can be accessed in only certain states of consciousness. Some people claim they can access the Akashic Records through dreams, trance, meditation, or near-death experiences, but these methods are usually hit or miss. American mystic and psychic Edgar Cayce is an example of someone who claimed he had successfully read and used the Akashic Records. It is true that various techniques and spiritual disciplines, such as yoga, pranayama, meditation, prayer, and visualization, can be employed to quiet the mind and achieve the focused preconscious state necessary to access the Records. This can also be done if one has the right psychic abilities (as Edgar Cayce did). For our purposes, however, we will use the Sacred Prayer given to us by the Mayans. As we will see, it is not enough to simply read the prayer. We must prepare carefully and keep an open heart in order to connect to the Records and receive the information.

Akasha has formed a part of many ancient belief systems. Numerous ancient cultures and socio-religious groups talked openly about the Akashic Records and claimed to have accessed them, including east Indians, Moors, Tibetans, Bonpos, Egyptians, Persians, Chaldeans, Greeks, Chinese, Hebrews, Christians, Druids, and Mayans. Sacred texts and manuscripts tell us that the ancient Indian sages of the Himalayas knew that each soul, or *atman*, recorded every moment of its existence in a book, and that if one attuned oneself properly, one could access that book. In India today you can see Nadi palm leaf readers. The belief is that Lord Shiva imprints recordings of the Akashic Records onto palm leaves, and that each human has a leaf on which the recordings of his or her soul path and progression are inscribed. Perhaps the Nadi leaves are a physical aspect of the Akashic Records. In Hindu mysticism, Akasha is the actual substance on which events are recorded. It is also what the basic elements of nature—earth, fire, water, and air—are made of, the membrane that envelops everything in the universe, and the substance that holds everything together in the essence of love.

Nostradamus claimed to have gained access to Akasha using methods derived variously from the Greek oracles, Christianity, Sufi mysticism, and the Kabbalah. Other historical personages who claimed to have consciously used the Akashic Records include Alice Bailey, William Lilly, Manly P. Hall, Rudolf Steiner, and, of course, Edgar Cayce. Many students of metaphysics believe that the Vedas, the oldest scriptures of Hinduism, and Sanskrit, one of the oldest languages, were extracted directly from Akasha. According to acient Egyptian texts and scrolls, those who could read the Akashic Records in Egypt were held in high regard and would advise the Pharaohs on their daily activities and dream interpretation. The high priests and priestesses from the Mayan tradition imparted the Akashic Records to the people to help them bring their energy and knowledge to a much higher realm. As previously mentioned, it is through the Mayan tradition that we have received the Sacred Prayer.

The Urantia Book, a compendium of spiritual and philosophical writings by the Masters and angelic beings, confirms the validity and reality of the Akashic Records in several parts of the texts. Indeed, Paper 25 states, "The recording angels of the inhabited planets are the source of all individual records." The Urantia Book discusses God, Jesus, science, cosmology, and religion, and is said to be a book of destiny. It was first discovered around 1924 and its main objective appears to be to reveal higher truths and thereby expand the consciousness of the reader.

Alternative names for the Akashic Records include:

- Book of Life (Christian—Philippians 4:3, Malachi 3:16, Revelation 3:5, 3:8, 3:17, 8:20–21, 8:27)—"In the last days these books shall be opened."
- Cosmic/Collective Consciousness
- Cosmic Mind
- Universal Mind
- Nature's Memory
- Universal Library
- Book of Remembrance (Jewish)
- Hall of Learning
- Hall of Knowledge
- Repository of Thoth (Egyptian)
- *Der Bewusstseinsraum* (German; roughly translates as "the room of conscious knowledge of yourself")
- Akashic Chronicles
- Etheric Records (Tibetan)
- *Anima Mundi* ("soul of the world")

Many people have a linear way of thinking about the Akashic Records. They visualize them as existing in a grand library or an etheric temple, a place where records and scrolls are kept. In a way this is correct, but they are much more than that. Looking at Diagram 1 on page 28 you can see the word *Akasha* on the far right with an arrow pointing up and down. This represents how Akasha is everywhere, the connective tissue that holds the universe together, much like the connective tissue in our own bodies. This connective tissue can be found in the tiniest of cells as well as the largest bones and organs; without it, our bodies would simply collapse. In the same way, Akasha is the connective tissue that holds the entire universe together, continuing into infinity. The most beautiful part about this is that the purest essence of Akasha is love. This means that if we learn to truly speak the language of love, we can impact not only our world but the entire universe! With the energy that flows out of our hearts from a healed space, we can give our beauty and magnificence to all worlds in the pure essence of love.

The triangle in the diagram represents the five planes of consciousness: the physical, astral, causal, mental, and etheric planes. We will explore each of these planes in greater depth further on in the book.

Learning how to access your Akashic Records will give you the opportunity to use the Records' energy and information on a personal basis. You will be able to ask general questions for problem-solving or for furthering your personal

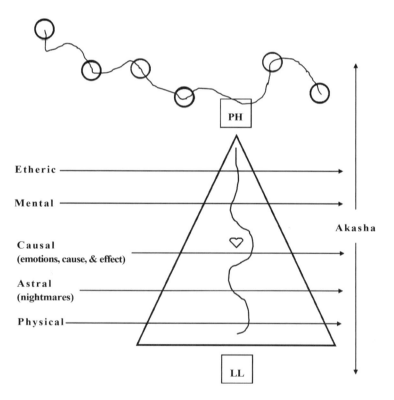

Diagram 1.

and spiritual growth. The healing energy of the Akashic Records allows us the freedom to choose grace in all things, overriding any illusion we have created that causes us to believe we are separated from Spirit. The material contained here comes from an ancient school of knowledge that will never bore you. As you enter into this mystery school and begin to study, recognize its potential and value in furthering your spiritual growth. You will be given information on ever-deepening levels, based on your openness and willingness as well as the relationship you develop with the Masters, the Record Keepers. Always act from your highest level of honesty and integrity. As you explore relationships and more, always ask for the highest good of everyone concerned.

The Akashic Records are one of the most powerful tools available on the planet today to help us remember our oneness with God and our own beauty and magnificence. One very important point to remember is that this process does not supersede any other spiritual work you are currently involved in, but rather will enhance it. Learning this material is working with the light for the highest good and looking to Spirit in a simple way for guidance, direction, and information. Your openness will determine both what you learn and how you use it.

2

What Can the Akashic Records Do for You?

The Akashic Records can provide unlimited guidance and are always available for inspiration in your life. Indeed, they are the guiding light that you have been looking for. It is as if someone handed you a magical crystal ball! If you simply look at it and trust it, it will provide an unlimited view of what your future can be like. It can guide you in making the right choices from the many that are available to you at any given moment. They function as a road map or GPS that can guide you on a long journey, giving you all of the details you need regarding where to turn, where to stop for food or rest, where to get gas so you don't run out of fuel—basically everything else you need to arrive at your destination safely.

Would this be of value to you? I am sure that your answer is yes! Know, however, that it will not be easy all the time. There will be issues that will surface from the past, because we have all been programmed not to trust, and I assure you that these issues will come up as obstacles to your progress. So just be prepared before you start your journey.

As we move through this material, you will learn invaluable information, the most important of which is the Sacred Prayer that has been handed down to us from the Mayan tradition.

This Sacred Prayer is what opens the portal of the Akashic Records. It creates the means for accessing your own Book of Life and establishing communication and a relationship with the Masters and Teachers, the Lords of Akasha. Later, I will discuss how I received the prayer, as well as other names given to the Akashic Records.

After learning the Sacred Prayer, you will learn Grace Points. These are points—energetic imprints—that manifest on either hand, depending on the nature of the issue that is being explored. If the issue has a feminine component, the Grace Points will show up on the left hand. If the issue has a masculine component, the Grace Points will manifest on the right hand. These Grace Points come from the Akashic Records. They are calls of action that help anchor the information we are receiving and help us let go of material accumulated in our emotional body that turns into ideas, thoughts, and beliefs that no longer serve us. We will explore Grace Points in greater detail later in the book. You will also learn one of the most powerful means of protection. The Sacred Prayer has a built-in segment that calls for the shield of love and truth to be placed around you; this is God's love and truth. The more inner light you generate, the greater protection you will need, and the Akashic Records will do just that for you.

Finally, you will learn how to use the energy of the Akashic Records with any other healing modality you may be using. If you are a Reiki practitioner, energy worker, massage therapist, psychotherapist, or medical doctor, you will be able to use this sacred energy with your personal practice to bring you to the next level of your personal potential. This does not apply exclusively to health practitioners, though. The Akashic Records can give you the inspiration to be a better communicator in any aspect of your life. You can mix the Akashic Records with just about anything you do. For example, if you practice meditation and want to bring your meditation to a much deeper space, you can open your Akashic Records when you sit to meditate. This will take you far deeper than before, and you will receive beautiful insights as a result.

The Akashic Records can be the most beautiful tool for bringing peace and resolution to troubled relationships, especially those with people who have already made their transition. Often we have a troublesome relationship with our father, mother, or another relative, but he or she passes on before we can make our peace with them. Depending on the severity of the issues, this person may or may not be able to make a full transition and allow his or her soul to rest in peace. Such people can become trapped on the astral plane in a holding pattern until they find peace and resolution.

When the time is right, when you are in the right heart space, the Masters and Teachers will bring that relative or friend into your presence so you can dialogue and make peace. When that soul is finally able to talk to you from a space of unconditional love, rather than a human space of fear and insecurity, it brings liberation to him or her. The result is the spiritual freedom to move to the schools of light and be prepared for his or her next incarnation. You will learn an easy way to connect, one that will take away the uncertainty of trial and error and allow you to go into your heart, open your Akashic Records, and be connected to Higher Source each and every time.

I often ask my students, "Have you ever tapped into the Akashic Records? Have you been there? How did you get there? What did you see? How do you know it was the real Akasha?" Many say it happened during meditation, during a dream, or when they were doing inner work that created an altered state of consciousness. They often see a beautiful, etheric temple in pastel colors with large pillars and a high ceiling; accompanied by the vision is an overall feeling of love and peace. Some see scrolls or large books bound in leather, which always appear to be very old. Others see a huge library where beings robed in pastel colors float around carrying these scrolls or books. They sometimes see angels placing the scrolls on shelves and transporting the information from the earth plane to Akasha. After hearing this, my follow-up question is usually "Can you return to this place you are so eloquently describing again and again, even two or three times a day? Can you access this realm at will?" The answer is always a variation on this: "No. It happens spontaneously and it is something I can't do with ease." The good news is that, with the Sacred Prayer, we can! You will be able to go to this place three or four times a day—or more—if you'd like. With this prayer you will have easy access to Akasha, where all the beauty, magic, peace, and love from the Masters will be waiting for you.

I call the Akashic Records the Library of Congress of the soul. Imagine, if you will, the actual Library of Congress in Washington, D.C., a huge place where you can find out just about anything. This library has many floors, and each floor has numerous discrete departments where you can go to obtain information; you can even go there to simply rest on comfortable couches, listen to beautiful music, and recharge your energy. Imagine the Akashic Records as a library just like this one, except it is far more beautiful, far more restful. Imagine a place where the moment you enter, you are greeted by Masters who simply radiate unconditional love. The moment you arrive, they are there to welcome you and guide you on an adventure of self-discovery through this "library." The information that you receive from the Akashic Records is meant to satisfy an innate need for knowledge about yourself and world around you.

This library of the soul, like many real libraries, is so vast that we must learn how to navigate it in order to best utilize it. One of the reasons we use it is to acquire information and knowledge. But this is not just static knowledge for knowledge's sake; the energy that is contained in the Akashic Records is, quite literally, transformational. It has the power to change, heal, restructure, and transform. If we are sensitive enough, if we can trust and believe that this subtle energy will heal, then we simply sit in the energy and allow the process to take place. The energy of the Akashic Records contains all of the ingredients needed for healing.

We are actually programmed from infancy to discover ever more information about ourselves and the world around us. Just look at what we build in almost every city: large structures dedicated to disseminating knowledge. We build colleges and universities, and people go to them because of their desire to acquire knowledge. The world presents us with myriad opportunities to learn and discover all the time. However, we learn best from personal experience. What we learn from books must be translated into practical life by adding an emotional component. Once that emotional component is present, the information is "coded" into our cellular memory and becomes permanent.

From infancy onward, we are perpetually creating new brain cells that will help us to identify the specific knowledge we are seeking. If we are learning music, for example, our brain must create the brain cells necessary to accommodate music so that we can identify the notes and symbols we read on the page. Likewise, if we are learning math, engineering, or a new healing modality, we must develop new brain cells that will help us identify that which we are learning. As we give our learning life, we attach an emotional component that will make it permanent.

I often give the following example in my classes. Imagine you are a toddler, just 2 or 3 years old. You see a candle flickering on the coffee table. The little flame catches your eyes as it moves; it looks as though it is dancing for you. Naturally, you go toward it and want to touch it, but if your mom is there and she will (hopefully) tell you, "No, don't touch. It will burn you!" You don't know what that means, really, so when Mom isn't looking you stick your finger in the flame. *Now* you know what she meant. You burned your finger so of course you start crying. You have had a direct experience—new knowledge—that carries with it an emotional component. You can now identify a flame as something that hurts if you touch it. You have satisfied your need to know in a very immediate and, in this case, painful way.

The information contained in the Akashic Records can be a very valuable source of not just knowledge, but direction and inspiration, in your daily life. Let's say you have an important meeting or presentation and you really want to shine. You know the material cold, but you also want to be at your very best. You want to be inspired, so inspired that you completely impress the people who hear your presentation and inspire them in turn. You want your auric field to be so full of love that they can feel it! If you expand your auric field to fill the room where you are making your presentation, everything and everyone there in the room will be touched by your field. If you fill it with fear, doubt, insecurity, and unworthiness, that is exactly what people are going to be feeling from you. In this case, your aura won't fill the room, but instead will probably reach just a few inches past the boundary of your physical body. If you open your Akashic Records and ask the Masters for inspiration, you can purpose-fully expand your auric field, just as if you were inflating a gigantic balloon, and "grow" it to the size of the room. You will be able to shine! (Hint: If you really want to shine brightly, fill your aura with the color fuchsia. If you want to project love, use pink; if you want to convey healing, use green. We will learn more about the use of these and other colors later.) Now you can walk into the meeting room feeling strong and confident, knowing that the Masters will be whispering in your ear. Now, the material will flow not just from your mind but from your heart. Fear will disappear, and you will be able to radiate an inner light backed by the most beautiful love of all, the love that radiates from the Akashic Records.

Another example: If you are a healer and want to increase your knowledge or create an entirely new system that will make your healing practice shine, you can ask for specific Masters that have the specific knowledge of the heal-ing technique you practice. If you are a musician and you want to be inspired, you can ask the Masters who know about your type of music to come and tutor you. If you have an interest in anything—alchemy, gardening, art, writing, me-chanics—ask the specific Masters to tutor you. If you want to create the most aromatic and heady blends of essential oils and want to know exactly which oils and how many drops of each to use, you only need ask for the Masters with that expertise to come to you and show you how.

With the Akashic Records, your imagination is the limit. The real question is, how much can you imagine? How much do you want to grow? How much do you want to shine? Imagine that the Akashic Records are as vast and end-less as the sky itself. Imagine that you are on top of the highest mountain in the world and you can see a full 360 degrees around you. You know there is more, much more, beyond even what you see, and you feel a hunger. You feel like an adventurer, an explorer. You are willing to take risks because you know that if you do, you will be increasing your personal potential. You know that you're worth it! Again and again I see the inspiration of my students skyrocket, once they understand they can move from the general to the specific.

What do I mean by this? Let's look at one of my students, whom I will call Christina, as an example. Christina came and took all three levels of the Akashic Records classes from me, and eventually she was able to hear what I was saying about the specific. You see, many times we have selective hearing and are unable to really take in certain concepts until enough detritus has been cleared from our conscious and subconscious minds, until we can open our inner as well as our outer ears. In any case, finally it dawned on Christina that she could ask the Masters who specialize in the mixed media art forms she uses in to tutor her. She asked them to teach her and show her how to bring her artwork to the next level, and that is exactly what happened. Christina's art was skillful and compelling before, but after she started using the Akashic Records, it took on an entirely new dimension. It was outstanding. After this breakthrough, she started exhibiting her work in galleries and making money.

Imagine that with every stroke of Christina's paintbrush, every piece of paper she crumbled, every mask that she made, she was infused with the love of the Masters, and it is this energy that fairly radiates from her pieces. When people see her art, they not only see what she is capable of producing with her talent, but also the love she receives when she is working. That energy will, in turn, radiate into the homes of the people who buy her art, so the Masters are working indirectly through her to bring this energy of love and peace into homes everywhere. Maybe, just maybe, because of this energy, the owners will run into someone who introduces them to the Akashic Records or meditation or spirituality. Maybe that someone will be you!

Another student, John, was a musician and composer who wanted to make money through his work, but for a long time he just couldn't make it in the business. After all, it's a competitive field, and there are a lot of great musicians out there. John started to open his Akashic Records to write his music, and, slowly, his inspiration started to change the style of his music. With this inspiration, the world opened up for him. He has since won several prizes for his music compositions, and he is now making money with his craft. There is nothing better than earning money doing something you love! Moreover, as his music reaches the ears of others, they will feel the essence of the Akashic Records emanating from each note.

As I've already mentioned, another important reason to use the Akashic Records is for personal healing. This is an invaluable tool for exploring, as deeply as you wish, any area of your life. Do you have a personal issue that you have been dealing with for a long time? Is there a pattern of addiction in your life? Is there a reoccurring pattern in your personal relationships that you have been trying to change? Do you have an addiction to food, alcohol, tobacco, or any other substance that you have been trying to heal, and it is just not happening? You may have tried counseling, psychotherapy, or hypnosis—maybe even all three of these and more—but the pattern is still there. The fact is that if we don't examine an issue all the way down to its root cause and bring the emotional component from that issue to the surface, it is like cutting a weed to the ground. We may feel good for a while because we don't see it, but when the right conditions appear in life again, like water and fertilizer added to the weed, it will come back to the surface and raise its ugly head again. We get triggered; we get emotional; and the issue or pattern is right back where it was, staring us in the face. The Akashic Records can take you to the root cause, and getting to the root cause provides the ingredients for healing. It is akin to pulling a weed up from its roots. With the roots removed, the potential for the weed—the issue—to grow back again is eliminated.

In our journey we are going to explore the art of questioning (and it really is an art). If you open your Akashic Records and ask a yes or no question, you will be given a yes or no answer. If you are ready to go deeper, however, learning the art of questioning is a must. It will bring you to that root cause I have been talking about. To that end, we are going to formulate a question, and as you answer, I will be giving you follow-up sub-questions. Based on the answers you receive concerning these sub-questions, you will most likely be able to create still other questions; *this* is where the magic is. These third-tier questions and their answers will give you the deep understanding you need. The Masters will always give you a formula to follow so you can reach healing and resolution for whatever it is you are working with.

A few years ago, a woman I will call Susan attended my classes and finished all three levels. Unfortunately, she was diagnosed with breast cancer nine months later. The doctor, predictably, suggested chemotherapy. When Susan went in for her first session at the hospital, she opened her Akashic Records. The Masters started talking to her, reminding her that she had a powerful tool at her disposal for healing. They told her to go back into her Records and trust the information they had for her. She told me later that it was as though she remembered every word I said during those classes, and she felt a sense of great peace and confidence. They told her what to do, step by step, in a very precise formula. Part of this formula was to completely stop chemotherapy, which naturally caused her to panic a bit, but then a sense of inner peace came over her. She followed the instructions she received step by step, and when she went back to the doctor a few months later, they found that her cancer was completely gone. The main point of this story is not that a miracle occurred (and indeed, not everyone receives this kind of miracle), but that Susan explicitly *trusted* what she received. She did not allow one ounce of doubt or fear to enter her mind.

Another woman named Kate came to my Level 1 class, and during the opening circle she broke down sobbing. She told us that she had been looking for a tool that would help her deal with life, and she had heard about the

Akashic Records and my classes. I just happened to be going to Northern California to teach the weekend after she had initially come across the information on the Internet and talked to her friend about it. She told us with great emotion that she had found a lump on her left breast the size of a golf ball. She had been able to feel it, and it had also been medically diagnosed with x-rays and a mammogram. Kate said she was ready to understand the origin of this lump and to heal it and let it go. She spoke with conviction, and the energy of her certainty was beautiful to observe and feel.

At the end of class, in our closing circle, I looked at her, and she began to cry, but the crying was different this time. She said, "Remember what I said at the opening circle about the lump in my breast the size of a golf ball? When I was palpating my breast this morning, as I do every day, I noticed that the size of the lump had been reduced to the size of a pea!" It was so beautiful to witness. She came to heal. She learned a tool, the Sacred Prayer; she trusted the information she received; and in two days, she found the healing she had been looking for.

A note on free will: Of course, not all of us are ready *at this moment* to open ourselves up to this knowledge. But know that Spirit and the Masters are very patient with us, and they give us complete freedom to exercise the greatest gift we have: *free will* to make our choices. They can wait another lifetime or two if you are just not ready to dive in and heal patterns that have surfaced from this or previous lifetimes.

↢

Now that we've discovered a bit about what the Records can do for you, we will need to explore the five planes: the physical, astral, causal, mental, and etheric planes. These planes are all part of our human experience, and we move in and out of them as we interact with one another and make our way through life.

3

The Physical Plane

At the bottom of the diagram of Akasha on page 28 is the physical plane, the densest of all planes. This is where we can touch and feel someone, where we can hold something in our hands, and where we have needs like eating and drinking that must be satisfied. In shamanism it is called the middle world, the world where we function, eat, sleep, and breathe. This is the plane where we learn all of our lessons, the schoolhouse we call earth. This is the plane of the visible, so no special talents are needed to be able to experience this world. Comprised of nature and all of its elements, this world is broad and vast. It is a beautiful place of existence where we come to play. The amount of enjoyment we get out of it is entirely up to us. On this earth we act out our karma. This is the plane of cause and effect. Here, as you give, you receive.

The physical plane is nature and mother earth, and it is within us all. It is so vast that we can explore her for a lifetime and never exhaust her possibilities and wonders. During the time we are here, it is important to get to know her, interact with her, and feel our roots deeply planted in her. The root of the word *physical* comes from the Greek word *physis*, which originally referred to the physical world itself—plants, trees, animals, mountains, oceans. From this came the Latin translation of the Greek as *natura*, and from *natura*, of course, comes nature.

There is much beauty in the physical world, so much potential here for us to embrace it and consciously fulfill our lives. Spirit gives us the opportunity to return to the physical plane one embodiment after another to fulfill our destiny, to balance our karma, to achieve enlightenment, and to embrace our magnificence. Our nature, our physical world, is a prime piece of real estate in the universe. Think about it. How many planets do we know about? How many galaxies are we currently exploring? Has science found a single planet out there that has the exact characteristics of our own, a planet with oxygen, trees, mountains, oceans, rivers? Have they found a planet with an ecosystem that sustains all of life, including those of human beings?

THE VARIED GIFTS OF PACHAMAMA, MAMA GAIA

How, then, do we identify with nature? Sadly, in most Western cultures, we don't. For the most part, we have lost our sense of nature. We don't have earth rituals that deeply connect us to the magic and the mystery of the earth. We live in cities where concrete is king, where glass and steel buildings pierce the sky, and where sometimes it is difficult to even *see* the sky. In many places in the world, mother earth cannot breathe. We are choking her with concrete and pollution, and in doing so we are suffocating ourselves. How can we possibly connect to nature if it is so removed from our life, and we are so removed from it? For many people, the beauty of the earth is a distant memory or something they occasionally see on television. It is so very sad that, in our culture at least, we don't have earth rituals to celebrate its beauty and magnificence! Very few people remind themselves daily that the earth is alive, that Pachamama or Mama Gaia is vibrating with life and sentience. We take her for granted. Fortunately she is available to us as long as we consciously open up to receive her every day. This is why it is so important that you ground yourself by walking barefoot on the earth. Feel the air and the temperature around you, and the energy from the earth moving through your feet. We should extend our gratitude and honor to this beautiful earth we call home each and every day.

Have you ever let yourself go so deeply into nature that you become one with it? Have you ever entered a cave and felt as though you were entering the womb of the earth? Have you ever felt as expansive and fluid as the ocean itself? We can learn so much from nature, if we consciously connect every day, if we stop to look at the movement of the leaves in the wind, observe a raindrop suspended for a few seconds before it falls, watch an ant make its way to its little hill, stop to listen to a bird sing, or melt into the water of a lake. We must take the time to walk on the earth that is alive under our feet, drink it in, and integrate it into our entire body. We have to take a few seconds to hug a tree and talk with the flowers and insects and blades of grass. We must dialogue with the wind and use it as a friend that will bring our prayers to oneness with the sky. We should talk with the mountains and sit quietly to listen, because they *will* respond. We have to learn to be still rather than going for the quick fix. We can feel the delicious interconnectedness of it all within us, feel the ecstasy of living, and recognize that this day we are living will never come back again. It reminds us to express our deep gratitude for the gift of the earth and life itself as we continue moving forward, consciously creating our future.

Deeply connecting with nature will deeply connect us to ourselves. You were born on this planet not only to work out your karma, but also to enjoy this beautiful prime piece of real estate in the universe. Devour nature and let nature consume you. Become one with it; in doing so, you will reawaken your ancestral roots and they will plant you very deeply in your experience.

The Akashic Records are a part of nature. You can go anywhere in nature, be it mountains, oceans, rivers, or deserts, to open your Akashic Records and have an extraordinary experience of communion and dialogue. Pachamama has so much to give us. She has been the record keeper for centuries and has seen it all for millennia; she has even seen *you* quite a few times before as you came across this life experience in the past. Go and ask for the spirits of nature to come to you, to nurture you, and to give you the opportunity to create an earth ritual like the ones that existed in the old days, a rite of passage ritual. If you have never had an experience like this, create it! It will give you a deeply connected feeling like you have never had before. By giving to the earth from your heart, you will help the earth heal from all the abuses she has suffered due to what we call "progress." An experience like this will change you. You will feel far more connected to life and to the beauty, magnificence, and abundance we have on this planet, this beautiful planet nested in the universe.

What, you may ask, is a rite of passage? In many tribal cultures, a rite of passage is the passage from one life stage to the next and involves a psycho-spiritual trauma, a death/rebirth experience. It involves both a loss and a gain for the individual and for the community. The initiate acquires new eligibilities and relationships but leaves behind old comforts and the familiar. The community gains a more mature member but suffers a diminishment in the cherished qualities that the neophyte once offered the community. For example, the community may be gaining the self-reliance of the adult but is losing the innocence of the child. Similarly, it may be gaining the wisdom of the elder or crone, but losing the activity and cultural creativity of the adult. A rite of passage doesn't actually turn a child or adolescent into an adult. Rather, it supplies the energy that the adolescent needs to turn the corner successfully, a corner he or she has reached only after a long developmental journey. A rite of passage is not necessary for someone to progress to the next developmental stage, but it can sometimes be a significant catalyst. It always provides the opportunity for the family and the community to celebrate and formally mark the transition.

So, give yourself permission to enjoy life. Identify with and embrace the beauty, exuberance, and abundance we enjoy on this planet. Feel the core essence of what makes this place go 'round and 'round, the core essence of love. Let mother earth surround you with love. Take it all in and let it go deep within your cellular structure to every bone, cell, and organ, to your blood and DNA. Become this love and then go out and freely share this inner quality with others. Once you acknowledge that you are limitless love, you can dole out as much as you want, because you can retreat to the Akashic Records and to nature to replenish at any time.

Let this connection and abundance of love show you how to live your life. Learn from nature, mimic nature, and you will see how even the most severe wounds will heal in no time. As unlikely as it sounds, you can even look to natural disasters for this. I live in South Florida, so I will use Hurricane Andrew as an example. Hurricane Andrew was the second most destructive hurricane in United States history. Andrew hit South Florida on August 24, 1992. We saw not only the destruction of homes and properties, but the extensive damage it caused to nature. I remember driving around looking at the devastation and feeling so much pain, wondering how things would ever grow back to be as lush and beautiful as they were before. I knew that buildings, homes, and other manmade structures would be rebuilt, but what about nature? I had never seen anything like this before. Little by little, however, the strength, power, and determination—the inexorability—of nature came through, and in a matter of three or so years, nature was back! In fact, she seemed to come back with even greater force and beauty than before. South Florida was once again a beautiful and luscious place with exuberant nature all around.

I share this with you because all of the hurricanes we deal with, whether internal or external, are part of life. How you respond to these difficulties is what can and will separate you from the mass consciousness of victim mentality. In truth there is so much you can do about it. Become like nature and rebuild after your own hurricanes with the guidance of the Lords of Akasha. You will see that, just like South Florida, you will be far stronger than before. I always say that you can only go as high as you have given yourself permission to go low.

If you are a tall oak tree, 100 feet high, and your root system is shallow, the first time the strong winds of change hit you, they will bring you crashing down.

Raising such a tall tree back up is quite difficult, if not impossible. Conversely, if your root system is both deep and wide, when the winds of change come, you will be able to remain steadfast and strong, immovable. You will become more like a sheaf of wheat swaying in the wind. You will be flexible instead of rigid, and that flexibility will give you the ability to handle and rebound from change graciously. You will know that you have Spirit on your side, guiding you and giving you inspiration as you move through life. Such are the gifts and lessons of the physical realm, and they are invaluable.

4

The Astral Plane

The next level is the astral plane. This is the more disquieting plane of nightmares, entities, and discarnates, ghosts and spirits that are stuck and have not been able to move to the light. If you end up here and you bring inner light with you but are not capable of containing it, you will become a target, and these entities will try to steal it from you.

It's important not to confuse the astral *plane* with the astral *body*. The astral body is a subtle body, or ether-like counterpart of the physical body. It is the intermediary between the soul and the physical body; it is composed of fine energy particles and is an exact energy duplicate of the physical form that it mirrors. This energy body is attached to the physical body, usually at the naval, by the silver cord. The astral body and the mind are capable of traveling together when the physical body sleeps. People who are capable of seeing auras usually see the astral body as an aura of swirling colors.

The astral body is the vehicle we use to travel in the upper world. In shamanism, there are three distinct planes or worlds; the lower plane or underworld, where the animal spirit helpers live; the middle world, the plane of our normal everyday experience (this is the plane you are aware of as you read this book);

and the upper world, the plane of the spirit guides and angels, which is below the upper, upper world where the Masters reside. So, if we are in deep meditation or if we project ourselves to someone as we do distant healing, we are using the astral body to travel in the upper world.

Many times spirits or ghosts that are trapped in the astral plane will make themselves known to you. This can happen in many different ways. You may see shadows, hear noises or footsteps, find objects that have moved even though you know exactly where you left them, or see lights turn off and on and doors open and close on their own. You may have a strong feeling of a presence in your home; you may even perceive a cold wind or a sudden drop in temperature. These entities want to get your attention. In most cases people are afraid of this sort of thing and don't know what to do, so they run away and ignore it, but this just makes things worse. I always tell my students to be cautious of the living, not the dead, because they can harm you; the dead cannot. The only thing these lost souls are looking for is your help. They know you now have a tool that can help them, and they want to be released. They want to be free so they can move to the light and process their most recent lifetime and karma.

Let me give you an example. Imagine a man in his mid-30s. He is happy and accomplished, has a good job earning $200,000 a year, and life is pretty good. He meets the woman of his dreams and they get married. She is a small-business owner and makes $350,000 a year. With their combined incomes, they have a life of ease and plenty. They have two children, a boy and a girl, who have rounded out their perfect family. They have a beautiful home (professionally decorated, of course) with a white picket fence, a dog, a pool, a BMW, and a Lexus SUV. Life is good!

On his daughter's birthday the family decides to have a picnic in the park. On the way to the park after leaving work there is a detour in the road. He ends up having to drive through a dangerous neighborhood, and suddenly, out of nowhere, gunshots: *bang-bang-bang!* The man gets caught in the crossfire of a shootout and dies. Before he knows it, he is looking at his funeral from above, fully realizing that he is dead. This man was not ready to die. He was enjoying the prime of his life and he had all he could possibly desire. He was enjoying his earth ride and out of nowhere he ends up trapped in the astral plane. Little by little, he turns into an angry ghost. The only thing he wants is to return to that which he once loved and is continuously looking down on. Luckily for this man, his widow understands that all the signs she is receiving—the cold spots, the lights switching on and off—are from her husband who is trapped in the astral plane and looking for help. Through the Akashic Records, she is able to liberate his spirit from the astral plane and send him on to his spiritual evolution.

All spirits trapped in the astral plane are looking down on the place where they came from, the physical plane. Many times, the Masters and Teachers will bring a loved one, close friend, or relative to you through the Akashic Records, so that you can have a dialogue with his or her soul, make peace, and liberate him or her into the light. Later, we will review prayers that will help make this process easier.

So, how do we help a ghost or entity that is trapped in the astral plane? It is relatively easy. First of all, we have to be open to feeling/sensing, seeing, and hearing the spirit. You can do this with your Akashic Records open or closed, but if you have them open, you will have the added protection of the Masters and Teachers. If for some reason you cannot open your Records, you will need to make sure you have a very strong shield of protection around you in case the entity becomes angry and wants to attack you. (For more on shields of protection, see Chapter 15.) If you have the protection of the Masters, nothing can happen to you, as you will be extremely well-protected. I hope you take the time to open your Records when you are in a situation like this.

Once you are in the presence of a spirit or spirits, the only thing you need to do is ask them to look up. If they do, they will see a white light and behind that light, the presence of family members who have passed on. They may also see the presence of a saint or sage from their religious belief. If they were Christian, they may see Jesus or Mother Mary. If they were Buddhist, they may see the Buddha, Lord Maitreya, or Padmasambhava. If they were Muslim, they may see Ibrahim, Al-Yasa, or Muhammad. If they look up into the light and feel the welcoming energy of their loved ones, they will let go of their grip in the astral plane. The problem is that many times that entity is stubborn and doesn't want to look up. Entities trapped in the astral plane are always looking down to the earth because that is where they came from, and they have an attachment to it. You may have some convincing to do. You can help them move along using one of the special prayers that I will share with you in Chapter 18.

At this point, I would like to discuss something that will tie into some of the other information I will be presenting in this book, mainly addictions, troubled relationships, patterns of interference, and entities. I would like to preface this by saying that this is very deep work, but as with any deep work the rewards are many. Perhaps you have been battling an addiction or some kind of negative pattern that seems to be holding you captive. The pattern involves falling into unhealthy, abusive relationships, feeling tired and drained all the time, or some other repeated issue that keeps you on the dysfunctional side of life. If at some point in your childhood or adolescence, you told yourself you would never be like your mother or father, and now it feels as though they were somehow manipulating and controlling your life, the negative pattern may have begun at the time of your conception.

If you have been battling alcoholism and you know that your father and grandfather were both alcoholics, or if you have been battling an addiction to cigarettes and you know that both of your parents as well as your grandparents were cigarette smokers, you probably have an idea of where I am going with this. Speaking more bluntly, if your father was drunk when you were conceived, during the sexual act the alcoholism entity was so present that it entered your mother's body like a dark cloud. As a result, not only was your father's addictive pattern transferred to you, but the very entity that is attached to alcoholism, as well. Whether you know it or not, you have been surrounded by this entity all of your life.

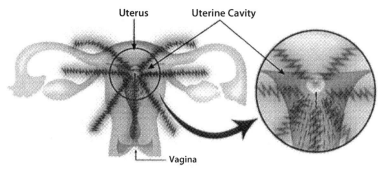

Diagram 2. Attack by an entity that is present at the time of sexual intercourse and conception.

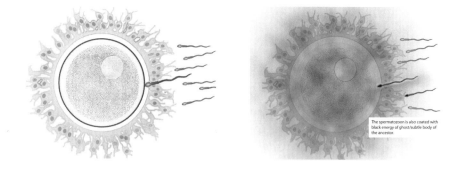

Diagrams 3a and 3b. A comparison between intercourse with and without the presence of an entity or ghost. a.) Normal, without interference. The union of sperm and egg in the absence of negative energy. b.) Abnormal, with interference. The subtle bodies of departed ancestors, entities, or ghosts create a *caul*, or shroud, of black energy at the time of union of sperm and egg, and gain control over them.

As ominous as this sounds, you don't need to be overly stressed out about it. Even if you've never been aware of this dynamic until now, this is a perfect and beautiful opportunity to bring resolution and healing to the issue. If you see the multiple threads connected here, like the tentacles of an octopus, you will be able to clearly see the many areas of your life where an attachment like this has been affecting you. Cheer up! Rejoice in the awareness. Through this book, you will be able to work with the loving energy of the Lords of Akasha to neutralize and even remove the imprint and send the entity back into the light. Heal and continue living your life dedicated to uplifting others as you become more aware of your own personal potential. In this way you will inspire the world around you, and feel the accomplishment of your connection with the Akashic Records.

We will talk more about addictions and dysfunctional patterns in Chapter 8.

5

The Causal Plane

The causal plane is the plane of emotions and of cause and effect. This plane is where most of the emanations of energy that we generate are stored. Think about it: If the causal plane is the place of emotions, what is the single biggest factor that carries us through life, causes us to do what we do, and teaches us most of our important lessons? Emotions! When we learn something merely at an intellectual level, over time we tend to forget it. When an emotional component is added to the learning process, however, it creates an imprint that will last throughout our entire life.

What does it mean that this is the plane of cause and effect? It has to do with the natural law of karma. There are certain cosmic laws that we humans have to abide by, and one of these is cause and effect. As you give, you receive; the energy you put out is equal to the energy that comes back to you. Every cause has its effect, and every effect, its cause. Everything happens according to this law. "Chance" is but a name for an event whose cause has not yet been recognized. There are many planes of causation, but nothing escapes this law. There are other laws we can't escape, such as the law of gravity. Maybe you can learn to temporarily balance your energy and levitate or become David Copperfield, but for the most part, you can't avoid gravity! There is also the law of vibration, which states that nothing rests, and everything is in motion. If you think about it, you will recognize that this law is a constant on this earthly plane. Nothing is static, from the tiniest cell in the human body to biggest wave in the ocean. Even things we see as static, such as stones or trees, are in fact always moving. The atoms in the stone and the wood are in constant motion to maintain the integrity of the whole.

The causal plane is a beautiful place where, with the help of the Akashic Records, we can become consciously aware of and balance our karma. By definition karma is neither good nor bad; rather, it is our actions that make it so. The more mindful we become and the more conscious and awake we learn to be, the more our karmic condition can change. We can then start eliminating negative emotions, judgments, beliefs, and pain. We can turn these things around and start accumulating positive merit. In doing so, we see our lives become more joyous, and we perceive life in beautiful, vibrant colors. We become one with nature, observing what is inside a raindrop and realizing it contains the whole ocean. We can become as small as an ant to explore the ground on which we meditate. We discover our beauty and magnificence. We start to fall in love with ourselves and with life itself. The most amazing thing is that we can't help but share this with others because this energy has to move, and its movement creates action from a deeply healed space.

CLEARING KARMIC CONTRACTS

As we've already discussed, the Akashic Records can help you understand and heal any repetitive or restrictive patterns that have emerged from trauma. This holds true even if that pattern's root cause is in a previous life. For example, let's say you have been dealing with an issue of money or lack of abundance. You work hard for your money, but seem incapable of holding on to it, as if you had holes in your pockets or your bank account had a leak. This can come from one of two areas of your life. One is a learned pattern from this lifetime, such as having had parents who were always struggling to have enough money and arguing about money. In this case, your issue has to do with a pattern set for you in this lifetime involving an imprint from your parents.

However, if this is not the case, your issue could be coming from a previous life. Perhaps you were a monk or a nun and you made a vow of poverty. In a situation like this, all of your basic needs were met by the church, and you were able to dedicate your life to devotion, meditation, prayer, and service. Perhaps you had chores such as working in a garden or caring for animals, but you didn't need to make money, and anything you did earn was given back to the church. In this situation, the vow that you made is like a contract, and you unknowingly brought that contract with you into this life. Because you are no longer a monk or a nun, this contract doesn't serve you anymore. The good news is that contracts are not permanent purchases, but leases; so you don't "own" your contract/vow of poverty, even though you brought it with you. With this understanding, and through the Akashic Records, you can explore issues like this one that are currently affecting your life and relationships. These issues could be anything from body pains with no explanation to karmic issues that have caused a troubled relationship.

Let me explain what I mean by our contracts being leases rather than purchases. All contracts that we make at a spiritual level run their course in a cycle on the cosmic clock. Each cycle of the cosmic clock begins at 12:01 and ends precisely at 12:00 of the next cycle. Perhaps you have noticed how some relationships, whether romantic, business, or familial, experience an energy peak. You know instinctively that you need to bring the relationship to an end, but fear creeps in, and you feel unable to do anything about it. As the energy peaks, it is as though it were 11:55, and you have those five minutes (though they may actually be five days, five months, or five years) to bring things to completion. Often, however, because of that fear, you don't, and once that clock turns to 12:01, you bring that issue into the next cycle, which could last six months or six years, depending on the pattern you have created. Those five minutes before the end of the cycle represent the critical time when Spirit is telling you that a contract is coming to an end, and asking you if you want to renew the lease or terminate it. With the awareness of this cycle, you will have the opportunity to explore issues like this one through the Records and bring them to completion.

THE SEVEN LORDS OF KARMA UNDER THE GREAT WHITE BROTHERHOOD

Once you become aware of an issue or issues that can be traced to a previous life, I highly recommend that you sit down and write a letter to the Lords of Karma. The Lords of Karma are beings who have taken embodiment on earth previously and have generated enough merit or balanced enough of their personal karma to earn their ascension. The Lords of Karma belong to a unique group called the Great White Brotherhood. Within that brotherhood is a special department—the karmic department—and the Ascended Masters who oversee this department are known as the Lords of Karma.

In the United States government we have the president, followed by the vice president, the secretary of state, and so on. There are also many different departments within the government, such as the Department of Transportation, the Department of Defense, and so on. You can view this governmental structure as a pyramid, with the president at the apex and everyone and everything else below. A similar structure exists within the realm of Spirit and the dimension that your soul resides in. At the apex, there is the Creator; to his left and right are the Lords of Akasha. Unlike the Lords of Karma, most of them have never taken embodiment, so they carry within them the greatest purity and love available. Right below the Lords of Akasha are the beings of the Great White Brotherhood. Within the Brotherhood there are many different departments with different beings in charge of them; one of these departments is the karmic board. The Lords of Karma are cosmic beings who have evolved through many eons to the point that they are perfectly suited to balance their own karma and arbitrate the karmic situations of others through their higher consciousness.

Here are the names of the seven Lords of Karma under the Great White Brotherhood:

1. **Cyclopea**: Also known as the all-seeing eye of God. He holds the immaculate concept of the divine plan of perfection for humanity's evolution.

2. **Great Divine Director**: He works very closely with Saint Germaine and will help clear all karmic debts through the absolution of all that is not of the highest divine truth and order for your being, no matter how great or small the debt may be.

3. **Goddess of Liberty**: Many recall her as the female angel who assisted them in choosing their parents and blueprint of their life. She also holds the balance for liberty and freedom for our world.

4. **Portia**: She holds the balance of mercy and judgment. She helps those who want to balance heart and head. She also helps those who judge and criticize others from the lower mind to raise their energy to their heart center so that they can be loving toward themselves and others.

5. **Quan Yin**: Known as the goddess of compassion, she is the eastern counterpart of Mother Mary and she works to balance the feminine energy.

6. **Pallas Athena**: The goddess of truth, wisdom, strength, strategy, crafts, and justice.

7. **Lady Nada**: She is the twin flame of Jesus. She works on the ray of compassion, governing humanity's development of the divine qualities of ministration, service, and peace.

In your letter to the Lords of Karma, write down the date and your full name. You should describe the information on this issue that you have received through the Akashic Records. Be specific. Describe the lifetime in question and, more importantly, the feeling or impetus behind the pattern you've been experiencing as a consequence. Write that you are now aware that this contract was made previously, that you are at the 11:59 hour of the cosmic clock, and that you are not willing to sign the lease again. In doing so, you are bringing the contract to termination. Once the letter is finished, seal it, put it in an envelope, and write a title on the front of the envelope, such as *Termination of the lease contract in relation to my finances.* Put it on your altar.

It is important to be note here that every pattern within us, even if it is negative, holds a certain amount of weight within our psyche. The psyche doesn't tolerate imbalances, so if we do not replace the resulting empty space with a new energy, there is a danger that the wisdom of the psyche will bring back the same or a similar pattern to occupy that empty space. This means that we have to consider what it is that we want to occupy our psyche right after we let go of something. This always reminds me of the prayer of St. Francis of Assisi:

Lord, make me an instrument of Thy Peace
Where there is hatred...let me sow love.
Where there is injury...pardon.
Where there is discord...unity.
Where there is doubt...faith.
Where there is error...truth.
Where there is despair...hope.
Where there is sadness...joy.
Where there is darkness...light.
Oh Divine Master, grant that I may not so much seek
To be consoled...as to console.
To be understood...as to understand.
To be loved...as to love.
For it is in giving that we receive.
It is in pardoning that we are pardoned.
It is in dying that we are born to Eternal Life.

I interpret the last line in two ways. The first is literal death and the opportunity of the soul to enter into a space of Nirvana. The second is that certain aspects of the self—patterns, additions, and co-dependencies—must die as we enter deeper into our spirituality and in order for us to continue moving in the direction of spiritual enlightenment. I think the words of

St. Francis resonate with absolute truth in people's hearts and minds. They are powerful words that can help us replace something that we have let go of with something of equal "weight" but much greater value. Our psyche will not only tolerate this new information, but every cell in our body will rejoice as we continue doing this work.

Next, write another letter, this one to the Lords of Karma, following a similar format as before. Write the date and your name, and give the letter a title such as *New lease contract in relation to my finances*. Then, with the help of the Akashic Records, write down exactly what you want. Be specific. Do *not* just write that you "want abundance," because if you have created a pattern of abundance problems, what you will get is an abundance of problems! If it is money you want, don't be afraid to say so and to name the specific amount. Above all, be realistic, and don't venture outside of your personal potential. For example, if you ask for a million dollars in just one or two years, and that amount is completely beyond your ability to create, you are basically canceling out the contract as you write it. On the other hand, if you write that you would like to create $75,000 in 18 months, and that amount is within your ability to create, you will likely reach that goal. Remember that you can review your contract at a later date and expand it if you wish. In a way, this whole process is not only rewriting your karma, but also retraining your mind to see new potential. Remember that you can rewrite this contract as many times as you wish. However, you will need to take the time to allow the new contact to "settle" in your conscious mind so that it can imprint your subconscious with the new information. If you start ending and beginning contracts too often, you will create a pattern of distrust.

Once you finish the details of the contract, date it, sign it, and *give it a due date*. This is important because you don't want to bring this lease into your next life. This could limit your personal potential in your next life, depending on the merits you accumulate in this one. Once this is done, put the letter in an envelope, write the title on the front, and put it on your altar. You want to burn the old contract as soon as possible. Do this outdoors so the smoke can be carried by the recording angels and delivered to the Lords of Karma. The best thing to do is to create a bed of white sage, put the envelope on top of it, light it, and watch it be consumed as you completely let it go in the joy of the occasion.

After this, wait until the next new moon and burn the other contract in the same way. As you wait for the new moon, look at and acknowledge the new contract on your altar every day. In doing so, you will reinforce what you've written. If you wish, you may make a copy before you seal the envelope so you can read it every day. This will help give the right message to your psyche and start training your mind to the new contract information. Simply continue on with your life knowing that, yes, you will have to work to make things happen, but you will be able to see the ease with which change takes place as the result of clearing and bringing all karmic contracts to an end.

A WORD ON MERIT AND KARMA

At the moment we make a decision to experience life as an independent soul, there is a field of energy created to record every thought, word, emotion, and action generated by that experience. With this awareness comes great responsibility because we are either accumulating positive merit or not. The accumulation of positive merit is what will make our karma, and hence our life, easier. This is what, at the end of this lifetime, will determine the outcome of our next lifetime, so we want to take the opportunity to be conscious of our actions, making sure they come from the heart and with the essence of love and compassion. We want to eliminate any and all conscious and unconscious desires to harm others in any way, to remove criticism, judgment, and hatred from our lives, and to do whatever we can in this lifetime to leave a positive imprint on our lives and the lives of others.

I have mentioned merit and karma a few times. Let me explain the difference between the two. Karma is directly connected to the Law of Cause and Effect: As you give, you receive. This is fairly simple to understand. Your actions determine the type of karma you are creating or generating. Positive actions bring positive results into your life. Negative actions bring negative results into your life. Karma is natural law, not moral law. Every thought or deed will cause an effect and can therefore be called karma. Karma has nothing to do with a punishment or reward system; rather, it is a natural law that is always evolving toward balance as a whole.

Karma has three important phases. The first form of karma (*sanchita karma*) is in the seed state. This karma is dormant and has not yet started to mature; it is the sum total of accumulated karma from this life and all past-life actions. The second form (*kriyamana karma*) is the current, day-to-day karma that we create today by our actions, which are soon to become seeds. Consider that these latent seeds will eventually reach maturity and sprout at a future time, in this life or the next. The third form of karma (*prarabdha karma*) is the karma that has formed from mature seeds and is now active in our daily life.

Prarabdha karma is derived from the well of sanchita karma. It is the ripe fruit generated from the seeds sown from past actions. Of all three forms of karma, the third (prarabdha) is the one that we operate under in our daily life, and therefore the one we are most aware of. This karma manifests in desires, emotions, dependencies, aversions, insecurities, repetitive patterns, addictions, and, of course, family-related karma. Prarabdha karma is destined to run its course, but with mindful awareness one can reduce development of dormant seeds of karma that will reach the prarabdha state. Sanchita and kriyamana karma can be balanced and gradually exhausted or eliminated by living a diligently loving, faithful, sincere, honest, and devoted life. We can also refer to this kind of living as mindfulness or devotion—*Bhakti*—in which union with divinity is sought.

Our mental attitude is directly connected to the way we act in life, and it is the condition, or the essence, of our mind that imprints the karmic patterns that get transferred from one lifetime to the next. When we say we are dealing with karma from past lives, we are simply reenacting the mental patterns that created the original condition. When we become aware of this, we have the opportunity to clear the mental patterns or to balance that karma. Karma doesn't have a positive or negative blueprint; it is simply an open opportunity to create the mental imprint that is directly connected to our actions, actions that can be positive, negative, or neutral.

In a way, merit and karma are similar, or at least integrally related. The word *merit* can be defined as "the state or quality of being deserving or worthy of, to earn by service" (*Merriam-Webster's Dictionary*). Merit is the positive end result of positive actions generated in this or a past life, and is not in any way connected to negative actions. The more we act with kindness, love, compassion, and generosity, the more positive merit we accumulate. Merit has all the ingredients to bring our life to the next level of our personal potential, and will determine what our next lifetime or embodiment is going to be. Be mindful and aware of this, and work during your lifetime to accumulate merit.

The more we heal ourselves, the more we let go of our patterns of limitations, addictions, and co-dependencies; as we do this, the more we embrace our beauty and magnificence. The more we allow our divinity to surface, the more caring, patient, understanding, kind, and generous we will become. We let go of the governing actions of the altered ego and serve the world more often and with greater strength; as we do this, we generate and accumulate positive merit.

6

The Mental Plane

The mental plane is a sword with two very sharp edges. We need the mental plane, and it can be our greatest ally; but it can be our biggest enemy. The mental plane has the capacity to take us to the past, which it does quite well for most of us. It can also take us to the future, but the mind needs to be trained or it will go right back to what is familiar—memories from the past. If we can come to the point of truly understanding the function of our mind, we have tremendous potential to fabricate and co-create our future. All things that are a part of our reality are conceived by the mind, orchestrated by the mind, and created by the mind.

Mind is defined as non-physical. It is a phenomenon that has the ability to perceive, to recognize, to create experiences, and to react based on our environment. That which the mind is exposed to from our earliest years creates an imprint. In this sense the mind is like a multiple cassette recorder. When we are born, it gets turned on and starts recording. Some of what mind perceives and records is played over and over again. This creates patterns that many people spend the rest of their lives dealing with. For many people, mind is a prison, a torture chamber they cannot escape. This is why psychiatrists have such a booming business. They prescribe mind-altering drugs for just about any reason: If you are feeling anxious, here is a pill. To me this seems like a quick fix, essentially sedating people and having them behave according to the norms and rules of those prescribing the drugs.

The mind is divided into two main aspects: clarity and knowing. This means that the mind can be clear and formless and allow objects to arise within it. It is also an awareness of consciousness that can engage with objects. Because of this, the mind has the potential for self-liberation. These two aspects of the mind are both conceptual and non-conceptual. The conceptual is the normal mind, the mind we use every day to function and survive in daily life, the one that allows us to remember which car is ours and what street we live on. It helps us identify and understand the reality we live in. The non-conceptual mind is the pure mind, the mind that has the potential for self-realization and liberation. You may be asking, "Liberation from what?" I am referring to liberation from the entrapments the mind itself creates. Through clinging and desire, these obscurations make us unhappy, put us in a prison, and create the state of what I call "woundedness" with which so many people identify.

Woundedness refers to the state of the wounded self, the "poor me" that acts as the victim and is always in need of sympathy. This wounded stance can be seen in the person who, within the first 10 minutes of meeting you, has told you his whole life story and all the bad things that have ever happened to him. Perhaps the person is 60 years old and is still suffering from something that happened when he was 12 years old that he simply cannot let go of. The ego knows that by clinging to that endless cassette tape it can get sympathy, and it is much easier to be wounded than to be strong. More people are going to identify with the suffering and wounds of others because it makes them feel as though they are all in the same boat.

Now let us get back to the mind of infinite potential, the mind that is as vast as the sky and can attain self-liberation. Imagine a clear and beautiful day. The temperature is perfect, just the way you like it. You are able to go sit on the top of a mountain, and you have a 360-degree view of the sky. You see the sky's beautiful blue color. The horizon reaches as far as the eyes can see, and here and there you see clouds that come and go. Some are small and delicate like angel wings, and others are big and full. Some are even dark and pregnant with rain, and you know that at some point a storm is coming.

The vast beautiful sky is your mind and all the clouds are your thoughts. You can follow a cloud with your eyes as far as they can see, but eventually the cloud will disappear. If you learn how to train your mind, you can allow the clouds to gently and slowly fade into the vastness of the sky. Many of us create a chain of clouds, like a train with hundreds of cars behind the locomotive, yet there is always a space between the clouds. This space is the space of "no mind," and it is in this space that the potential for understanding the mind and for self-liberation live. This non-conceptual mind is just like the sky, and its fundamental essence is pure. I love Sogyal Rinpoche's statement, "It is the pure nature of the mind which has the potential to realize emptiness." This emptiness is the space between your thoughts. With training, understanding, and patience, the space between thoughts will be elongated and, little by little, you will be brought to the space of no mind. In the space of no mind, you can find peace and refuge. Here you can find the doorways to higher realms, self-liberation, understanding, and enlightenment.

Through the Akashic Records, we are afforded a real view into how our mind operates. We can look deeply at the dozens of cassette tapes that are playing in our subconscious mind. With that information, we have a choice. How do we achieve the stillness I am describing? We achieve it through meditation. Later I will discuss the three very important aspects of the Akashic Records, which I call View, Meditation, and Action.

7

The Etheric Plane

The etheric plane is part of the vital, life-sustaining force of all living beings. This energy is present in all life forms and is part of the natural processes of the universe. The etheric plane is the highest on our pyramid before we move out to the highest of planes, Akasha. The etheric plane is close enough to the physical plane for us to go there to find rest, rejuvenation, and healing. When we need to recharge, when our spirit guides come to help us, or when we feel lifted up by Spirit, this is the place we go. Many of the teachings that we receive during dreamtime or deep meditation come from the etheric plane. If, before you go to sleep, you ask your angels to take you to the temples of rejuvenation, they can take you to this plane to be tutored, nurtured, and healed.

The etheric plane is the doorway to a higher dimension, the exit point of the mental, emotional, and physical bodies. This is where the seventh charka can open up to higher dimensions. It is where we find our true connection to Spirit, stimulating connection to the eighth chakra and entrance into the higher dimensions, like Akasha. The eighth chakra is the entrance to the transpersonal realms. When we open our Akashic Records, we move our energy to our seventh chakra. As this chakra opens up, it allows for energy to flow out of the body and connect to the eighth chakra. The eighth chakra in turn receives the energy and gently opens up, establishing our connection with higher realms.

As our energy gets fine tuned, it is as though we move to a place that is higher than our bodies, and the Masters and Teachers lower their energy. In this way, we meet at the membrane that separates us. They do not come down to our level as spirit guides do. The Masters will come down as far as they can, but they expect you to go up as high as you can to meet them. The eighth chakra is that meeting point. From there, the energy, soft like a cloud or a mist, will go up as high as you let it. The Masters will take you as high as you are willing to go.

One good thing about the etheric body is that it has enough distance from the physical, mental, and emotional body to be somewhat autonomous. Nonetheless the etheric body is still a part of the four lower bodies, so it can be impacted by them and them by it. The etheric plane is where consciousness goes to rest. We experience an increased freedom from the constraints of time and space, giving us the ability to experience greater amounts of freedom. The etheric body really can travel beyond time and space!

The etheric plane is where you can meet other individuals of like energy and vibration. When you feel deeply connected with others, this is precisely how the connection is made. I am sure many of you can identify with the following statements: "I was thinking about my friend Sally and then she called!" or "I was putting my energy into meeting so and so, whom I have not seen in many years, and then we randomly bumped into each other!" Where does the energy go that allows these kinds of connections to take place? It goes to the etheric plane. If you practice or have received Reiki, long-distance healing, or any other form of healing, the etheric plane is the space where you connect and the avenue where the energy travels.

Here is another good example of the workings of the etheric plane. Let's say you have a strong desire to go somewhere. Perhaps you find out about a spiritual retreat, such as the Akashic Records Intensive in Bali, and you feel this is a place where you want to go to deepen your connection with Akasha. Once the acknowledgment is made and the strong desire is born within you, you will likely start "feeding" the goal with the energy to bring it into reality. That energy goes to the etheric plane to make it happen, especially if you bring the desire into your meditation. Remember, energy flows where your attention goes.

Consciousness creates far more experiences than we are able to process in any one given day. The etheric plane serves as a buffer to counterweight the energy that mind creates, so we have to be extremely grateful for this plane. We have to nurture it like a baby, teaching it how and where we are going to use it for our highest personal outcome.

Addictions and Addictive Patterns

As we continue observing the diagram of Akasha, we see two small boxes: one below the bottom line of the triangle, with the letters LL, and the other at the very top, above the apex of the triangle, with the letters PH. The box that you see at the bottom of the triangle with the letters LL represents the lower level.

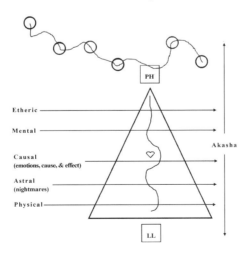

This represents you at the most basic level, the physical level, the level from which all opportunities arise. From here we start moving in all directions in the triangle. We explore the physical plane and all that it means to be alive. This is where we satisfy all of our basic needs like food, drink, clothing, and shelter. This is also the plane of Samsara. I will explain the meaning of Samsara in the next few pages, and what this means in terms of addictions and their power over us.

I believe it is worth taking time here to explore addictions and addictive patterns because it is so easy to fall into the trap of addiction. The Akashic Records can be an amazing tool to explore our mind and discover the causes of addiction; once that discovery is made, the Masters can help you in finding the solution.

Let us first understand what an addiction is in mundane terms. The Diagnostic and Statistical Manual IV (DSM-IV) describes addiction as a "maladaptive pattern of substance use, leading to clinically significant impairment or distress as manifested by three (or more) of the following, occurring at any time in the same 12-month period:

- Substance is often taken in larger amounts or over a longer period than intended.
- Persistent desire or unsuccessful efforts to cut down or control substance use.
- A great deal of time is spent in activities necessary to obtain the substance (e.g. visiting multiple doctors or driving long distances to purchase it), use of the substance (e.g. chain smoking), or to recover from its effects.
- Important social, occupational or recreational activities are given up or reduced because of substance abuse.
- The continued substance abuse despite knowledge of having persistent or recurrent psychological or physical problems that are caused or exacerbated by abuse of the substance.

Tolerance is defined by either:

- The need for markedly increased amounts of the substance in order to achieve intoxication or desired effect; or
- A markedly diminished effect with continued use of the same amount.

Withdrawal is manifested by either:

- The characteristic withdrawal syndrome for the substance.

➔ Taking the same (or a closely related) substance to relieve or avoid withdrawal symptoms."

Many people consider addictive behaviors such as gambling and alcoholism to be diseases, but others consider them to be behaviors learned in response to the complex interplay between hereditary and environmental factors. Still others argue in favor of a genetic cause. Some researchers point out that, unlike most common diseases such as tuberculosis (which has a definite cause and a definite treatment model to which everyone agrees), there is no conclusive cause or definite treatment method to which everyone agrees for most of the addictive behaviors.

Regardless of the cause of an addiction—whether it was caused by a learned behavior brought about by peer pressure, by the observation of the overuse of alcohol by an addictive parent, or by the influence of alcoholic grandparents— perhaps you are now battling the addiction yourself. It doesn't really matter where the addiction came from. As long as you take it to the feet of the Masters, as long as you bring it, with an open heart, to the altar of the Akashic Records, you can have a solution for the problem.

Spiritual research indicates that 96 percent of addictions are due to ghosts, entities, demons, devils, negative energies, or departed ancestors. As I mentioned previously, the seeds of addiction are introduced into the womb itself by this entity, energy, or ancestor. Due to the spiritual nature of the cause of addictions, only spiritual remedies can successfully alleviate them. Here is where the Akashic Records come in. When we finally become aware of a situation like this (and keep in mind that the energy is very subtle and may take a while to unfold), the best way to make it known or get it to rise to our awareness, is through the use of the Akashic Records. This is because of the dialog that can take place with the Masters in order to uncover what is so deeply hidden and affecting our adult lives.

There are two types of addictions in life: negative and positive. A negative addiction is exemplified by the heroin addict, the habitual smoker, or the gambler. A positive addiction, on the other hand, can manifest in the marathon runner, the meditator, or the adept yoga practitioner. The mechanism of addiction is the same in both cases. If you are an alcoholic, you will miss booze if you don't drink, and you will miss it tremendously. The same will happen to you if you become positively addicted. If you run every morning for one hour, and then one day you are unable to run for some reason, you'll feel sad and depressed, as though something were missing. In many cases there will also be a feeling of guilt.

If someone who is will-oriented (by this I mean someone who is gifted with tenacity, drive, inner strength, and conviction) becomes negatively addicted,

Root causes of addictions

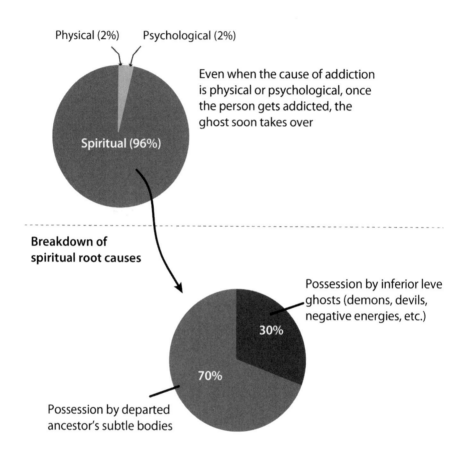

Diagram 4. The root causes of addiction.

his life will likely be wasted. If he becomes positively addicted, however, he will become a great creator. The addiction mechanism is the same and the mind is the same, but the outcomes, of course, are completely different. If you can start working on positive addictions, you will experience tremendous benefits. For example, if you want to cultivate a positive addiction to meditation, choose one meditation practice or technique and put all of your effort into it. The effort has to be consistent and regular. Persistence and continuity is the key.

A tricky negative addiction can occur when a spiritual person becomes addicted to a spiritual high, which in turn generates a pattern that creates an altered ego. Because it is difficult to repeat a transcendental spiritual experience, the person starts feeding the memory of what happened by talking about it and by creating feelings of grandeur, feelings of being "better than." The danger here is that the person will not only miss the experience of real Truth, but will use the addiction to feed the altered ego. A spiritual experience that is transcendental in nature is like receiving a hit from a powerful drug—it leaves you speechless and in awe of what just took place. As soon as you have an experience like this, naturally you want more; you want to own it, keep it, and repeat it again and again. The intellectual component of this kind of addiction is the belief that if you just had enough of these experiences, you would feel great all the time. That's the mindset of an addict: "I got it and I lost it. I don't have it. I need it."

Some common types of addiction:

- Alcohol
- Drugs
- Food
- Gambling
- Internet
- Nicotine
- Prescription drugs
- Sex/porn
- Shopping
- Work
- Gym
- Text messaging
- Telephone
- Facebook
- Spiritual high

Symptoms of addiction:
- Resentful attitudes
- Risky behaviors
- Aggressiveness or passiveness
- Mood swings
- Physical symptoms (weight gain or loss—using food as a drug to calm the storms)

↝ Nervous twitches and ticks

↝ Reactive behavior instead of proactive behavior

↝ Always feeling overwhelmed

↝ Anger if not able to check email, text messages, etc.

↝ Not trusting one's feelings

↝ Never feeling good enough

↝ Depression

↝ Anxiety

↝ Lethargy

↝ Guilt

The cycle of addiction and codependency requires three main groups of people:

1. The enablers: Those who allow/excuse/finance/bail out the addict.

2. The persecutors: Those who stir the pot in order to put the addict on the defense and look for a way out of the pain.

3. The victims: Those who wallow in the excuse that someone is abusing them/picking on them/insulting them/not recognizing their good qualities.

In the normal cycle of addicted relationships, the enablers, the persecutors, and the victims occupy all these roles at various times and to varying degrees. The fact that people switch roles makes it very difficult to assess anything until a crisis occurs. Many times the person addicted will feel lonely, like there is no support around him. Hopefully, if we are exercising a pattern of addiction in our lives, we can recognize it and use the Akashic Records to find the solution. The love and support that come from the Masters and Teachers can help a great deal. Hopefully, we will also find a group of like-minded individuals, a *sangha*, as a support system. Sangha is a Sanskrit word that means an association or assembly, a company or community with a common goal, vision, or purpose.

ADDICTIONS AND LIBERATION FROM SAMSARA

In the Buddhist ideology, *Samsara* refers to the cycle of birth, suffering, death, and rebirth. Samsara also means continuous flow. It directly refers to re-incarnation. The Buddha taught that one can overcome attachment to Samsara and the suffering that occurs in living a human life. We can experience liberation in this lifetime from the attachments we develop, as well as the ones that life has for us. How do we begin to liberate ourselves from Samsara? The best way is to begin understanding what these attachments are and how they affect us in just about every part of our life. We need to see how these attachments create fear, distractions, and, yes, addictions.

The Akashic Records are a great tool to begin this process of understanding. They can lead you into a deep inner exploration of the self and, in doing so, help you understand how Samsara operates in your life. Mindful practices are also wonderful tools to support you as you continue working with the Akashic Records. Practices such as meditation and contemplative prayer can help liberate you from attachments and bring you to a state of *Nirvana*, transcendence from attachment.

The more you work and develop a relationship with the Akashic Records, as well as other mindful practices, the more you will experience nourishment and comfort in being in the energy of the Masters and Teachers. You will be filled with inner power, joy, and enthusiasm to continue moving forward on your journey. You can expect a wonderful sense of peace that comes and takes over your life, as well as an experience of your heart opening to love more and more. You will feel love for yourself, love for others, and love for life itself, and this love will open the doors to wisdom and compassion. Together love, wisdom, and compassion can transform any situation that you are presented with in life—even addictions.

What creates this grasping, this attachment that I am talking about? The ego is the source of all self-grasping, self-cherishing, and self-absorption. These three are the root of all suffering and all hard-heartedness. The ego is a fragment of the psyche observing the rest of itself from a psychological distance, but at the same time infiltrating the whole. We actually need the ego to operate in life, but we need a healthy ego, not an altered ego. If it weren't for the ego, we wouldn't wonder about our true place on this earth. We would simply take it. It is our ego that does the wondering. Without ego, we would take our place instinctively, as every other living creature does.

Our ego gives us the sense of being human. What is so great about being human, you may ask. Perhaps it is our ability to know. This gives us the ability to know ourselves and the ability to fall in love with everything, including the mysteries. If we are the only beings to consciously *know that we know*, then we are the only ones who can admire the universe as a universe and consciously know our place in it. Without conscious self-awareness, there would be no one to appreciate the universe and creation.

This earth is the plane where we experience being human, and our consciousness (as opposed to that of any other living creature) makes a difference because we have the ability to know that we exist, that we are a part of the planet, of life, and of the universe. This human experience gives us the ability to experience feelings and emotions and human love and be conscious about it. As humans, we have the awareness and consciousness to know that we have the potential to become anything we want to become.

This is different than the lion and the gazelle, which only have the potential to be that which they are. We, however, have the potential to embody our magnificence. We cannot only search for that magnificence within ourselves; we also must traverse this world with the most wonderful gift that we have received from Spirit, the gift of free will. If we are the only beings that know that we know, we are the only ones who can admire the beauty and the totality of the earth and the universe. You can say that this plane is the schoolhouse of life. Depending on our karmic merits as well as our inner desires, we explore the other planes that are illustrated in the diagram of Akasha. Based on our inner desires, we create the conditions and circumstances in life, based on the law of attraction, to be exposed to the right teacher or teachings.

Referring back to the diagram on page 65, the box with the letters PH on top of the triangle is the penthouse; the box at the bottom with the letters LL is the lower level. I view the two boxes, the LL and the PH, as if they were two floors connected by an express elevator. We enter the elevator on the ground floor and we exit where the doors open at the very top, the penthouse. As we shall see later in this book, the Sacred Prayer *is* the express elevator, and once you enter, as long as you don't change the wording of the prayer, you will bypass all of the other planes and end up at the apex of the pyramid. You could say that this elevator has only two buttons, LL and PH, and it will not stop on any other floor. Once you arrive at the penthouse, the doors will open to the entrance of the Akashic realm, the library of Akasha, the Library of Congress of the soul, and the Masters will welcome you. You will immediately feel a shift. It may be a very slight, subtle shift or a very forceful and noticeable shift; but either way, don't create an expectation about how it will feel to be there or the way you will perceive the energy around you. All you need do is be open and feel the love and compassion that will flow from the Masters.

From this point, this spiritual penthouse, you will be able to proceed into the library. As I mentioned before, you can choose to simply sit in the energy and receive its healing power, engage in conversation with the Master that greets you, or be very specific in naming what it is you want. Depending on your line of questioning, the right Master will show up to guide you on your journey for that particular session. In this way, you will have the help of the Masters as you face any patterns of addiction in your life. What a powerful tool you have at your disposal!

Troubled Relationships

*M*any people have unwieldy and distressing relationship issues that are all tied up in karmic family dynamics. Sometimes we carry these issues with us until the end of our life. Earlier, I talked about departed loved ones who come through the Akashic Records to find peace with us so that they can continue in their spiritual evolution. If someone assumed the role of aggressor in your life, he or she will most likely need to come back to you through the Akashic Records and make peace with you. If you are the one who is holding on to anger or resentment, you have a wonderful opportunity to make your peace with that person, whether he or she is alive or not. Of course, the best time to do this is while the person is alive! Holding onto resentment is like drinking poison and expecting the other person to die.

You can gain deep understanding about these types of relationships when you realize that many times, in the spirit realm, a contract is created between you and someone else. The contract may have been for that person to be as negative or nasty as he or she was so that you could learn the lessons that are available to you. In other words, many times you will encounter people who have come to sacrifice a portion of their lifetime—or their whole lifetime—just for you! This is done out of the purest love that anyone can possibly share with another. With this love comes the possibility, based on your understanding and personal spiritual evolution, to liberate both yourself and that other soul.

It may be that you have an agreement with that soul based on previous lives together and, because of the merit you have gained in previous lives, you both know at a soul level that you will come across and embrace your *Dharma*, your spirituality. If you have been close to the Akashic Records in the past, you will come across the Akashic Records in this lifetime, as well, giving you the opportunity to balance the karma between the two of you. Your actions and understanding can liberate you and the other soul so that in his or her next incarnation, he or she can come closer to his or her own Dharma. Think about this person's actions as a testament to his or her supreme love for you; think, too, about the sacrifice of the suffering and pain the aggressor must have felt at a soul level during this lifetime. Many times such a person will pass on and simply sit in limbo in the astral plane, waiting for you to come to this realization. This understanding brings many to tears and to their knees in gratitude for the supreme love that this individual had for them. Speaking more personally, this understanding helped me to heal my troubled relationship with my mother, and it made me see and appreciate the huge sacrifice she made for me in her lifetime. With this understanding, I was able to release her and all the attachments we created together, so that she could move freely into her next life without the karmic ties to me holding her back. I am so grateful for this powerful and beautiful understanding!

I have mentioned the word *Dharma*; let me explain what it is in greater depth. Dharma is the natural law or the order of things as they revolve around and interpenetrate with your life. It is the central concept in Indian and Buddhist philosophy, in the context of personal obligations or duties. It also refers to the religion or path that a person chooses. Dharma, as it is understood from sacred texts, is a divinely instituted order of all things; and human happiness, harmony, and social justice depend on how well the individual lives his or her life following the natural law of Dharma. It is believed that if the individual follows and fulfills his or her Dharma, he or she will proceed more quickly toward personal liberation.

Many times it is essential to write a letter to the person with whom you have had the conflicting relationship. You will learn how to use the Akashic Records to do this, asking the Masters and Teachers to guide you as to what is the best thing to write. Writing a letter is taking a thought or series of thoughts and making it into something more concrete. This is helpful for the following reason: When you say something to someone, she will interpret what you say through her own filters and, depending on how full of negative emotions she is at the time, what you say may or may not enter her field of understanding.

However, if you write a letter and you make your points nice and clear and concrete (you can create bullet points to define each point you need to convey), she has something she can read again and again to facilitate understanding. Furthermore, if you imprint the letter with the energy of the Akashic Records and with the essence of pure love and compassion from your heart, it will be the first thing that comes out when she opens the envelope. If this person is still alive, it is the perfect time to do this. Once she passes away, however, the ball-game is completely different. If you have something to express, the time is now!

Make sure you don't use e-mail or text messaging as the means of communicating with this person. Show her the respect she deserves, and write the letter by hand, perferably with blue ink. This shows that you have put your heart, hand, and pen into the action of writing the letter. When you write this letter, make sure you don't make it about her; instead, focus on you and your feelings. Refrain from any name calling, insults, or unnecessary talk about bad times that you have had together. And anyway, if you have your Akashic Records open to write the letter, name calling or insults will not be a part of what the Masters give you.

Here is a set of helpful letter-writing guidelines:

1. Make sure the letter is hand written with blue ink.

2. Consider carefully the words you choose. Use your Akashic Records to guide you (more on this in Chapter 18).

3. Avoid writing when you are experiencing feelings of negativity or anger. Use the Akashic Records and Grace Points to clear your energy first. I will explain Grace Points in greater detail in Chapter 20.

4. If the relationship is over, be clear on that. Give the person the opportunity to understand your point of view so she can move on.

5. Make the letter about your feelings and how the relationship has impacted you.

6. Express your gratitude for the lessons learned. Write the letter with love.

7. Be positive about your future as well as hers. Use words and phrases such as *in gratitude*, *thank you*, *best wishes*, and *many blessings*.

8. Sign the letter with your first name. *Do not* close the letter with "love" or "yours." Doing this implies that you want to get close to the person you are writing the letter to, and it is best to be neutral. For example, use the salutation "Peace" and then your name, or simply sign your name without a salutation. Again, the Masters will guide you in a better way.

10

Forgiveness

I would like to talk about forgiveness for a moment. Lack of forgiveness holds people back, keeping them frozen in a memory from the past. It hardens the heart and keeps you from being able to love and be loved in totality. A lack of forgiveness will sully just about every relationship you have, and it will hold you back in your spiritual progress.

Almost everyone, if they have lived long enough, has been hurt by the words or actions of another. Perhaps your mother criticized you constantly, perhaps your partner had an affair, or maybe a business partner betrayed you. These wounds can leave you with lasting feelings of anger, bitterness, and even a desire for vengeance. However, if you don't practice forgiveness, you may be the one who is continually getting hurt by continuing to live in the past. By embracing forgiveness, you embrace peace, hope, gratitude, and joy and move with ease into the future.

Forgiveness is essentially a *decision*—a decision to let go of resentment and thoughts of revenge. The act that hurt or offended you may always remain a part of your life as a memory, but the energetic imprint of that action doesn't have to. Forgiveness can lessen or completely erase that emotional imprint, which will in turn create the room for you to be able to focus on other aspects of your life. Forgiveness will lead you to new feelings and emotions and will leave you with a greater ability to understand and have compassion for both the one that hurt you and yourself.

Forgiveness doesn't mean that you deny the other person's responsibility for and ownership of his actions. It doesn't justify wrongdoings. In forgiveness you become fully responsible for your own actions and reactions to the actions of others, and you give the other person the opportunity to do the same. Even if this person is no longer on this earth, we are working with energy, so healing can take place with help from your Akashic Records. You can forgive the person without excusing the act. Forgiveness brings peace that will help you go on with life.

On a personal note, about 10 years ago, I was working on issues of forgiveness. These issues went all the way back to my mother and included other subsequent relationships that failed me. I was exploring forgiveness in relation to all the romantic relationships that I have ever had. Talk about a handful of work! Working with the Akashic Records, the Masters asked me, "Out of these troubled relationships, what have you learned?" Immediately my mind rushed to all that I have learned from each one of them. Then they asked me to make a list of what I had learned. Following this, they asked, "How do you feel whenever you learn something that makes you grow, both as a man and spiritually?"

I immediately answered, "It makes me feel good. I am always open to learning about myself."

They then asked me to identify an emotion that makes me feel good. As soon as this was asked, it was as if the floodgates that contained a waterfall opened up. I was showered with pure, white, liquid light that enveloped my entire body so intensely that I almost passed out. I lost track of time as I basked in the magnificent feeling of gratitude.

When I came back from that experience, the Masters were right there waiting to continue the conversation. When they asked me how I felt, I answered that I felt clear, free, empty, and loved. At that moment, I realized that gratitude and love are like brother and sister, and when one is developed, the other one follows. The Masters then asked me, "If you feel gratitude and love from what you have learned, then what is there to forgive?"

My answer was, "Nothing."

By falling into that deep space of gratitude for the lessons I had learned and the transformations that had taken place, the need for forgiveness melted away as love, gratitude, and compassion took over. I saw that, for me, a greater capacity to love and live a life of freedom emerged. I continue working with gratitude today as I move into my future.

Here are several benefits of forgiveness:

- ↬ Healthier and happier relationships
- ↬ Greater spiritual and psychological well-being
- ↬ Less free-floating stress, hostility, and anger
- ↬ Lower blood pressure
- ↬ Fewer symptoms of depression, anxiety, and chronic pain
- ↬ Lower risk of alcohol and substance abuse
- ↬ Increase in physical strength
- ↬ Immune system boosting
- ↬ Better digestion
- ↬ Relief from self-sabotage
- ↬ Friendlier, more tolerant state
- ↬ Peace of mind

11

Fragmented Pieces of the Soul

Let's now explore what is above the apex of the pyramid in the diagram of Akasha. Notice the little circles connected with a squiggly thread. These circles represent fragmented pieces of your soul. We all have soul fragmentation. When we experience trauma,

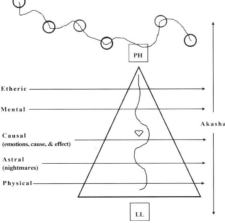

a portion of the soul often gets disconnected so we can cope with the situation. There are countless ways in which soul fragmentation takes place: rage, grief, an accident, being spooked, distressing arguments, injury, surgery, and so on.

Here is an example. Imagine you are a 6-year-old child and you are home playing with your favorite toy. Mom comes along and tells you that you have to go to the supermarket with her, but you are so immersed in playing, you don't want to go. Mom tells you that you have no choice; you can't stay home alone. You grab your favorite toy to come along, but Mom says you can't bring it because it's distracting and you'll only be gone a little while. You bring a smaller toy instead and keep on playing in the car. Mom parks and you are now crossing the street, holding Mom's hand and playing at the same time. You accidently drop your toy, so you let go of Mom's hand and take a step back to pick it up. Out of nowhere, a big truck comes flying down the street, and before you can do anything, you hear the loud horn of the truck, look up, and see the truck is only 10 feet away from you!

At that precise moment, a big truck is coming your way and you know on some level that this could be the end of your life. It doesn't matter that you are such a small child. We all have that built-in mechanism that tells us, "Danger! Watch out!" As you see the truck coming your way, you experience fright, a big "Ahhhh!" comes up from the depths of your stomach and your heart, and you feel paralyzed and frozen. As this happens, in order to cope with the upcoming danger, a piece of your soul disconnects.

Mom notices it all and acts like a super-mom, as moms tend to do in situations like this. She reaches out, grabs you by the hand, and pulls you to safety; as she does, you reach out and grab your toy. Your heart is pounding in your chest as though it's about to jump out altogether. Unfortunately, that is not all that happens. Now your mom is scolding you because she told you not to bring the toy and you disobeyed. You end up with two traumas, one from almost being hit by a truck, and the other from the severe scolding and possibly a spanking from your mom. This example shows how soul fragmentation unconsciously and automatically takes place.

Let me give you another example. Now imagine you are a young teenager, and you are very much in love. This is the first time you have fallen in love, and the person you are with means the world to you. Remember what that felt like? It feels as though you are being literally consumed by this world of love and fantasy, a first love so strong and so passionate. Unfortunately, things change and start deteriorating, and before you know it, you are constantly fighting and arguing. The final straw that breaks the relationship is an argument that leads to full-on rage. In that experience of rage, you lose complete control, and when you do, a fragment of your soul gets disconnected so you can cope.

Here is another example for you. You are now in your mid-40s and you just left a great party where you had a fantastic time. You are heading home and it is raining quite hard, so you are being as careful as you can as you drive. However, it is dark and wet, and your vision is not as great as it used to be. You are driving on a two-lane highway, and as you enter a curve, you see the headlights of an oncoming car. This vehicle has lost control and is heading your way! You react as fast as you can, stepping on the brakes, and your car spins out of control. As this is happening, you experience stark terror for your life. You see that, in a fraction of a second, you could be in a serious, even fatal accident. You then experience a soul disconnect, and this is what helps you to cope with the trauma. Luckily, your spirit guides and angels are there by your side, and the accident is completely avoided.

If you don't fully recognize that you experienced soul fragmentation at that precise moment, at some point in your future you will have to do what is called a *soul retrieval* to bring it back. If you do recognize that a fragment of your soul was disconnected, then at that precise moment, you can actually call it back to you. It is as if the piece of the soul were a balloon connected to you via a silver cord. In that moment, you are still holding on to the end of the cord, so it is relatively easy for you to pull it back before it continues moving away from you and out into the abyss.

All kinds of situations can disconnect you from your soul. Severe grief is a major one; losing someone you love dearly can take you to a very similar place. Losing control of your mind, for a variety of reasons, can also create a soul disconnect. If you have at any time in your life used psychedelics and had a bad trip, you can basically assume that there was a soul disconnect. Drinking alcohol to the point that you completely lose control, and finding yourself wondering what happened the next day, can be another situation that prompts soul disconnect

THE DISOWNED SELF

Let us now turn to the *disowned self*, the part of the self that gets fragmented only during childhood. In this case the disconnect is not so much a result of severe trauma; rather, it comes from the close family dynamics during the time we spent growing up at home. The disowned self can be found in the mystical child, the rebellious child, the intuitive child, and the adventurous child:

The **mystical child** is the part of you that, at an early age, saw and spoke to angels, spirit guides, and unseen friends. Perhaps you shared this experience with your parents or grandparents, and at first it was considered cute, but as you got older, you were told to stop playing and having silly conversations with imaginary people. Little by little, you accepted what your parents told you and you stopped your communication.

The **rebellious child** (one of my personal favorites) is the one who was innocent yet loved to get into trouble. This is the part of you that loved to do mischievous things, thinking that he was never going to get caught. If you are thinking that *my* rebellious child did get caught and, as a result, got into trouble and was disciplined, you'd be correct. In my case, my parents threatened me by saying that if I didn't stop misbehaving, they were going to send me to a military school. (Instead, they sent me to a boarding school where I got into even more trouble!) For a girl, the rebellious child could have been the one who played with boys and climbed trees while still wearing a dress. Her mother may have noticed and scolded her, "You are a young lady and should not climb trees, especially with a dress on. Better come inside to learn how to cook and be a lady so you can get married to a doctor."

The **intuitive child** was the part of you that had a highly developed sense of intuition. It was the part that knew what was going to happen before it happened. At first this ability may have gone unnoticed, but over time, it may have unsettled and even spooked your parents. So perhaps they convinced you to let it go, not to trust it. They may have even told you that this nonsense was similar to you hearing the voices of your imaginary friends.

The **adventurous child** is the part that loved to go everywhere—creating her own adventure, feeling the excitement of risk, and loving every minute of it. Did you ever sneak out of the house when your parents told you not to? Did you go with friends someplace you were not supposed to go, thinking you weren't going to get caught? If your parents found out, perhaps they grounded you or meted out some other form of punishment.

As you can see, anything you did during your childhood that was not supported by your parents or family and got you into trouble, sometimes repeatedly, contributed to your disowned self. This disowned self has been waiting for you to reintegrate her into your life. Through the Akashic Records you can explore these issues and see how they surface as a pattern of interference. The reality is you have a wonderful opportunity to recover and reintegrate these pieces of the self. This work is similar to the inner child work that many of you may have done. The most important thing about this work is that once that missing piece is integrated, you must give it life! Whatever that integrated piece tells you to do, you do it. In this way you return to childlike innocence.

There are many aspects of the Akashic Records that make it a powerful tool to learn about ourselves. The more you know about yourself, the better you can serve others, the happier and healthier relationships you will have, and the better your life experience will be. Many people are so desperate to know about themselves that they give their personal power away to others or to objects of prediction. There is absolutely nothing wrong with consulting an astrologer, tarot card reader, or psychic every now and then, but when this becomes a crutch, and when an individual cannot exercise his or her free will, then it becomes a problem. This is a way to leak energy that otherwise can be used for something creative and magical.

Wanting to know ourselves is nothing new, of course. *Know thyself* was actually inscribed on the walls of the temple of Apollo in Delphi in ancient Greece. It is believed Socrates was one of the first to make this credo a guiding rule. There are three ways in which the Akashic Records can help us look deep within to get to know ourselves. I call them the View, Meditation, and Action. These three elements are absolutely essential when we begin to establish a relationship with the Akashic Records, and practicing them can give us a direct understanding of how to create action in our lives.

One of the things that we have been programmed to do (based on our cultural dynamics) is to react rather than act, so we become reactors rather than action takers in our lives. We react to everything, and many times the reactions are adverse to the desired outcome. We react to what other people say, to the way other people drive, to what other people wear—food, manners, personalities, pain, stress, life! I firmly believe that 10 percent of life is what happens to us and 90 percent is the way we act—not react—in response to those circumstances. Our attitude and the way we act is what shapes the way we relate to others and to life itself. All of this is connected to a belief system. Many times that belief system is a wrong one that has been passed down to us from generation to generation. In many ways it is attached to our genealogy; indeed, this is a beautiful area of exploration within the Akashic Records.

That said, to me, attitude is more important than facts. It is more important than the past, than education, than circumstances, than failure, than success, and certainly more important than what other people think or say or do. Attitude is more important than appearance, giftedness, or skill. It can make or break a friendship, a home, an organization, or a regime. The remarkable thing is that we have a choice every day regarding the attitude we will embrace for that day. We cannot change our past or the fact that people will act in certain ways. We cannot change the circumstances and conditions that life presents us, the cards we are dealt, but we have complete control of our attitude and the actions we take in response to what is presented to us. The information presented to you here, with the help of the Masters and Teachers, will provide a wonderful way to change your attitude and behavior and move you into action rather than reaction.

As I mentioned previously, there are three aspects of the Akashic Records that can be used inside or outside of the Records in order to fully integrate and embody the information you receive. This process of integration can be a lifelong one. By "inside the Records" I mean sitting with your Records open. This may be a 15-minute visit or an hour-long process in which you are in communication with and receiving from the Masters. Outside of the Records, you sit to digest the information and allow the process to take place, just as we do after a fantastic meal: We rest, assimilate, and digest. I will review these three aspects—the View, Meditation, and Action—in depth the next few chapter, but I'm sure that their names are already cluing you in to what they mean and what they will do for you.

PATTERNS OF INTERFERENCE

Patterns of interference are one of the most important topics of this book and perhaps the most critical to understand to effectively access the Akashic Records. I can guarantee that when you open your Akashic Records you will encounter a pattern of interference on more than one occasion. There will be times when there seems to be no response from the Record Keepers, despite you doing everything right, including rephrasing the question and asking for clarity. Being aware of this is very important. You should not try to force an answer to flow, but instead closely pay attention and ask the appropriate question in order to gain clarity. Many times patterns of interference surface as an opportunity to be aware of the pattern itself; recognizing what is behind the pattern and causing it in the first place is precious information.

There are different ways of addressing these patterns. First, we have to know whether what we are experiencing is an internal pattern or an external pattern. If this is an external pattern, it is relatively easy to correct. If the experience is an internal pattern, it still represents an opportunity for resolution. In this case, you may want to use one of the other prayers in Chapter 18 to see if it helps lift the pattern. These prayers include a forgiveness prayer, a prayer for releasing outside influences, a prayer for loved ones and entities, and a prayer for personal clearing.

When you open your Akashic Records, first check to see if you correctly opened them. Opening them correctly means that you are truly present as you read the Sacred Prayer, not thinking about dinner or your boyfriend or some other distraction. If you know you were in a heart-centered space and that you were present during the reading of the prayer, then you can ask, "Am I experiencing a pattern of interference? Yes or no." This is a very direct question that will allow the Masters to give you a simple yes-or-no answer. If the answer is yes, ask, "Is this an internal or external pattern?" And then trust the answer you receive!

If you find you are dealing with an external pattern, close your Akashic Records and pay attention to your surroundings. Is the neighbor's dog barking? Are children outside playing and screaming? Is someone in your house banging pots and pans in the kitchen? Are there big electrical towers nearby emanating electromagnetic radiation that you can almost feel? All of these can be causes of an external pattern of interference and are relatively easy to correct. Simply wait until the noise is gone or change locations. Once you see that the environment around you is calm, you can center yourself and reopen your Records.

If it turns out that you are dealing with an internal pattern of interference, you may want to ask if the pattern has something to do with the fragmented self or the disowned self. If you get a yes, ask which one. From this point on, you can use the Akashic Records to start exploring the inner child and all of its intricate components.

12

The View

When we open our Akashic Records, we encounter the possibility of accessing what I call the View. The View refers to our being given the ability to see things the way they really are. In this place of clarity we can learn to realize the absolute state of our mind and know that all other distractions are merely games that we have allowed the mind to play. Here we learn the true nature of our mind because we enter into a space where there is no judgment or criticism. We enter into the space of compassion and love, a love so big it can melt away all past pain and sorrow. When we access the View, we can comprehend the naked reality of everything that is contained within us, of sensory perception, and of phenomenal existence—the extraordinary realm from the beyond which cannot be viewed or entered unless the mind is so completely open that it may see the inner space of true manifestation.

We can clearly see the difference between Samsara and Nirvana. In Samsara we are completely full of everything that makes up the human experience—thoughts, ideas, things, cultures, religions, politics, addictions, intolerance, anger, and more. Samsara is the cycle of pain and suffering that is present in everyone's life, until the moment we are completely liberated and free from all of these distractions. This process of liberation may take several lifetimes. In Nirvana we can experience an exquisite emptiness out of which the potential to Be, Do, and Have everything in our lives comes. This delicious emptiness brings us to the ultimate realization of peace, peace so profound that we can rest in our natural way of being. Ultimately, we realize that we can bring this emptiness and peace to Samsara, to life, and continue living in this world by being "in the world but not of the world." We can have a goal for our lives that is bigger than ourselves. We can then ask ourselves daily, *What can I do to impact the life of others in a positive way?*

At the same time, we experience the full realization that the View is the perfect way to learn, to be compassionate and loving, and to give ourselves all that we need in order to be comfortable in this ride called life. The View can help us Be, Do, and Have in the right order. You can be the person you always wanted to be, do whatever you wish to do, and have all that you desire, free from ego grasping and manipulation. From this space you can share the full essence of who you are with others. The society we live in believes that having is more important than doing, that we must have in order to do, and only as a result of having and doing can we then be. So we go in the order of Have, Do, and Be, and this could not be more wrong. If you have fallen into this trap, it is a great time to exercise the View and see that it is actually the other way around: Be, Do, and *then* Have. If you change your mindset, you change your reality; and if you change your reality, you change your life.

The best way to impact life in a positive, loving, and constructive way is to have a very clear view of one's life, one's path, and the way one lives it. We have to ask ourselves, *What am I doing every day at a conscious level to better myself, to heal, to let go of the past, to look at my life as an observer and see the drama that I am involved in?* Drama in life starts at a very early age and originates with our family dynamics. We buy into this drama, and as we grow up, the drama continues developing. We start responding in a robotic way to family, friends, authority figures, and the pressures of society. We learn that we have to conform to the views of others, that to be accepted by our peers we have to be like them. We learn that we must conform to belong.

If we have the spark of spirituality within us, we begin feeling uncomfortable. We start looking around and realize we don't belong in the groups we are conforming to. Sometimes we even recognize that we don't really belong to the family we have chosen to be born into. This self-realization is all part of the View. And this is not just about family dynamics. As we progress and grow, we continue to feel uncomfortable trying to fit into the materialism and consumerism of our society. We know there is something bigger. We continue searching and, as we enter the spiritual world, we start learning that we no longer belong to the values that we once embraced in our past.

For many people this brings a sense of relief, and they begin creating conditions and circumstances in life that support their growth and change. At the same time there is often a sense of struggle as we start changing and creating separation from family and friends. People who know you may not want you to change. They may want you to remain as you are, static in your milieu. They will fight you; they will try to convince you; they may even try to bribe you to remain a member of their club. Prepare yourself for the fact that the moment you start changing because of your newfound spiritual values, many if not most will start disliking you.

The good news is that if the separation is not radical, and such people are not completely out of your life, they will be able to see you change in a positive way. They will see that you are not as wounded or as needy anymore, that you have grown strong and embraced a more holistic, more spiritual, kinder, more tolerant, more loving, more grateful, and more compassionate lifestyle. They will see you become more empowered and secure, more successful and free from addictions—basically, more loving, happier, and at peace. As this positive change is observed, they will want to know what got into you, what are you doing that is creating this new you. You are, in fact, creating a new you by being able to see your life clearly through the View, followed by Meditation and Action. Don't be surprised if those who once judged and criticized you because you left their circle start coming to you for advice. You can become the way-shower, the leader who gives them a hand in starting their own processes of self-transformation.

The Akashic Records will give you the ability to clearly look at your life, at the conditions and circumstances that *you* have created. Personally, I see what I have been describing to you as a theatrical play. You are not only the main actor, but the director, as well. Many times, we don't even know we are the director and that, as such, we have the ability to change the script. Use the Akashic Records to get a crystal-clear view of your play. As you are sitting in the Records' energy, imagine that you can project yourself as a member of the audience watching the play with no attachment. You can also project yourself up and above your body and look down at the drama unfolding below. (I happen to like and often use the first image. I like to see my life as a theatrical play and take the director's chair as I observe the past unfold to the present.) Knowing that the events and circumstances of your life create your reality, knowing that your entire reality is a reflection of the way you have trained your mind to think, it is relatively easy to rewind and see your past. Change your way of thinking and create the reality, the life you want to live. A positive mental attitude goes a long way.

The ability to clearly see the past is one of the best tools the Akashic Records has to offer us. If you can view the past without attachment, you can make changes to the script. Ask yourself, *How am I acting? How about all of the other people involved in the play? Are they playing their parts in ways that are supportive to my life, my growth, and my spiritual evolution?* If not, you, as the director of the play, have a right to tell them that you are not satisfied with how they are playing their roles. You have a right to tell them they have to change their acting, and if they refuse or are incapable of doing so, you have a right to fire them. This part can be tricky because of the attachment they may have to playing their roles in your life. You have to be a strong director and be clear about the role that each individual ought to be playing in your life.

In viewing your life in this way, you can make changes to the imprints of your past and change the script as you move into your future. Remember that the future is not already written. It is determined by the choices you make in the present. It is written by you, the director. As you review your life, you may come across negative experiences from the past, and you likely think of these experiences as the bad parts of your life. The truth is that negative experiences are blessings in disguise. As you view them, try not to react to them with anger or aversion, as you might normally do, but instead recognize them as merely experiences that are a part of the drama, the play of your life. See them as illusory and dreamlike. The recognition and acceptance of these experiences will change their "charge," the pull they have, and liberate you. Ask for the guidance of the Masters and Teachers. This level of communication inside the View can be the source of many blessings and give you a very distinct direction in your life.

The View will allow you to know the true nature of your mind. The true nature of your mind is the true nature of reality, and this in turn is absolute truth itself.

13

Meditation

There is no better way to digest and understand the information we receive from the Akashic Records than through meditating. Meditating or sitting can bring the View into crystal-clear focus. In sitting, we can understand the information received. We can empty our mind of the distractions that get in the way, and realize the gems we receive from the Masters when we have our Akashic Records open.

Meditation is a technique that can help us go deep within the self and from that stance have a better understanding of ourselves. There are many forms and styles of meditation, but the ultimate goal is to take us to emptiness. In this space of no mind, everything stops, vanishing into the vast ocean of our minds just as the clouds vanish effortlessly into the sky. The space between thoughts is beautiful. It is the space where the mind rests from the process of thinking and attachments. This space can be developed as we deepen our meditation; and as we do this, the space is continually elongated. Between thoughts there is emptiness, and within emptiness there is the potential of everything. Meditation can help us empty our mind, and once empty, fill it back up with whatever we decide to put there.

The concerns that occupy the mind during our waking hours are active all the time. If we learn to empty the mind of all the dysfunction, drama, pain, and destructive memories from the past, as well as all lack, limitations, behaviors, and patterns that keep us continually experiencing life in the way that we do right now, we change our reality. If we are still identifying with family dynamics, constantly working at healing old relationships and being unable to move into complete freedom, meditation can be just the right thing to do after we experience the View.

If the goal of meditation is to empty the mind, how is it beneficial to take the information we receive from the Masters into our meditation? It is beneficial because it enables us to distill that information and take the next step into action. It is as if you were taking your thoughts and simply allowing them to be like the clouds in the sky. Imagine sitting in a meadow and looking into the vast, empty sky. Before you know it, a cloud appears, and then two or three, and perhaps eventually an entire chain of clouds. You simply sit there, observing each one as it passes by. If one remains in your sight, you allow it, observing it as something external to you. You may even want to dialogue with it and extract information for your own understanding, but you do it as an observer and not a participant. In doing so, there will be a moment when the cloud simply disappears, vanishes into the vast sky of your mind, and you can rest in emptiness. When the next cloud appears, you repeat the process again.

In this way we can say that meditation means to rest, undistracted and undisturbed, in the View. Meditation is being attentive to the information being received, free from any mental constructions, while remaining fully relaxed, without any distractions or preconceived ideas regarding the outcome. Meditation is about naturally being absorbed and assimilated into the silence, the emptiness and inner void that brings us to a space of peace, and at the same time a space of inquiry and mindfulness that can make us completely aware of the totality of our being. Is the space is where "mind observes mind," where I, the witness, can separate from my body, the mind of the mediator, and, from a completely neutral point of view, observe life as it is lived. This is essentially the process of projecting your mind outside of itself and then making a "U-turn" to observe the self. Meditation is also the natural flow that comes after the View. We receive the information and then simply take it into the silence. We are not *trying* to understand the information; we are simply observing, allowing it to be there, sitting in the energy.

When it comes to meditation there are a few points to remember. When a thought has come and gone, there is a gap where the past is already gone and the future has not risen, and so within that space exists huge potential. This potential becomes even larger if we learn how to elongate it. We can rest in this space of pure luminous light and awareness. It is inevitable that another thought is going to appear, and when this happens we need to maintain focus and attention on the information we are receiving. If we allow our ordinary mind to take us to ordinary thoughts, we have lost a precious moment of opportunity. If we are able to recognize this and stay focused, we slowly start recognizing the true nature of our own mind. As thoughts arise, we simply observe them and let them go, and as they go, they are liberated. Remain as the observer, feeling the peace of liberating thoughts.

This can be a very rich experience that will come to validate the information you receive from the Akashic Records in many ways. However, it is a practice that requires dedication and time. Many people in our culture have been programmed to accept the "quick fix." They want it fast and they want it now. You must remember that we are talking about the mind, which is similar to the sky. There will be days of heavy rain and many dark clouds, just as there will be sunny days with a few beautiful, fluffy clouds dotting your field of vision. All thoughts produced by the mind are capable of creating your reality.

You can also say that the mind is no different from the ocean, sometimes shallow, and many times so deep that you cannot see the bottom. It may be an ocean that is warm or ice cold, with small playful waves or destructive tsunami waves. It may be like a lake, a calm mirror belying the tremendous activity going on below the surface. In the stillness of meditation, we can take the storms and the heavy rain as clues, using them to have a better understanding of ourselves. This can be the food, the *mana*, of the awakening of understanding, and it is ultimately what we are looking for. We want to better understand ourselves and life itself so that we can heal and transform our reality.

It all starts with the information you receive from the Akashic Records. The Masters will introduce you to material that is already within you, the information that is going to help you be a better you. The Masters will give you many keys, keys that will unlock many doors to enter into deeper understanding and knowledge. What they are not going to do for you, however, is open those doors; that you have to do for yourself! You have to be willing to open the doors and walk through them, no matter what. You have to trust that if you are in your heart when you open the Akashic Records, if you have done the AAA recipe (which I will explain later), if you have not manipulated the information but kept it as pure as it is, then you will achieve greater understanding, inner peace, and knowledge.

The Masters have stressed the importance of bringing the View into your meditation to stabilize it. To accomplish this, first and foremost, you need to create the right environment, a place that is conducive to and has favorable conditions for your practice. This is not only valuable for meditation, but also important when you sit to open your Akashic Records. Removing yourself from the distractions of the world and your everyday environment is essential. How can you possibly create a permanent imprint that goes deep into your cellular level if you are attending classes from nine to five and at the end you go home to your computer, cell phone, and all the other endless distractions of life? You will not be able to do this if you go home to the bombardment of energy of others, of the city, or of a partner at home who is not supportive of your process and immediately deflates your energy. Imagine removing yourself from all of that and spending time completely immersed in the energy of the Records. This experience will change you, and will give you the tools to create similar energy when you live your mundane life. This is possible because you will have created an imprint at a cellular level.

Realize that there is no difference between meditation and the information we take from our meditation to everyday life. The integration of the wisdom received must be taken to your daily life and enlivened into action. We can call this the integration of wisdom and meditation, and it can help you to find the stability of your practice with the Akashic Records.

Practicing the View in mediation will allow you to have a constant flow of energy that will reinforce the information you are receiving. This will allow you to make changes and take action from a space of less involvement and greater wisdom; as a result you will see the conditions and circumstances in your life change.

In closing this segment on meditation, I leave you with the words of the Tibetan Master Nyoshul Khenpo:

> *Rest in natural great peace this exhausted mind,*
> *Beaten helplessly by karma and neurotic thoughts*
> *Like the relentless fury of the pounding waves*
> *In the infinite ocean of Samsara.*
> *Rest in natural great peace.*

10 reasons to meditate:

1. It makes you happier. Meditation actually floods your brain with happiness. Meditation brings a sense of peace and balance.

2. It gives you a stronger aura. Meditation fills your aura with inner light and strengthens the auric field. The Chakra system is protected from negative projections and negative vibrations. These vibrations can

come from the projections of others or planetary emanations and you can "avoid" unlucky events that can be draining.

3. It gives you more positive projections. Meditation increases your vibration and inner frequencies, so your projections become stronger, more focused, and more positive. Vibrating at a higher frequency will impact those around you in a positive way. Your communications can and will become clear and loving.

4. It helps you heal. There are certain types of meditation that include sound, intoning, or chanting. These sound vibrations help heal the physical body by projecting the sound to a specific body part, bringing organs, bones, and so on into vibration with a higher frequency.

5. It helps you gain focus. Meditating gives you discipline, so when you are working on tasks, your mind stays focused naturally. By being more focused, you will be able to accomplish more because meditation gives clarity of mind.

6. It helps clear your karma. It is not uncommon to bring karma from past lives into the present, in addition to the karma you create and accumulate in this life. By chanting certain sounds or mantras, you use the sacred words of the mantra to erase or move these karmic imprints from your field. When these imprints are transmuted, you are liberated and can move more freely in your life.

7. It hones your intuition. Meditation helps you to be more centered and focused. Meditation is like receiving a road map that will help you to fine-tune your energies. This, in turn, will sharpen your intuition. Intuition is a necessary ingredient to achieve your goals and keep heading in the right direction to your destiny.

8. It helps manifest specific intentions. Visualizing while meditating is directly related to the View. In other words, you can bring into the silence of your meditation what you observe in the View, thus giving you the opportunity to become an observer of your life. From this space it is possible to make your dreams come true.

9. It fosters miracles. Meditation will help to remove the density that is around you and bring you to a space of openness so that you will be able to manifest miracles in your life. Do you need a miracle? Don't ask twice: ask 108 times! Use a *mala* (a strand of prayer beads like a rosary) to repeat a mantra in order to manifest it.

10. **It gives you greater experience of self.** When you are meditating, you can discover multiple inner and outer dimensions, figuratively and literally. You can enter into a space of self-exploration, bring to balance your emotions and release them. You can explore the true nature of your soul, and you can fully integrate the View, Meditation, and Action with your Akashic Records.

Life is so much richer and deeper when you include the practice of meditation. Try it!

14

Action

Action is the creative flow that happens in our lives as the result of the View and Meditation. It is like a river flowing effortlessly to the sea. When this type of action starts permeating our lives, increased creativity, energy, and joy will result, as well as a greater confidence in who we are. We'll be more efficient in the use of our energy, creating a deeper connection with Spirit and the Lords of Akasha, and a greater and stronger relationship with the Masters and ourselves.

Action takes place as the result of the observation of our thoughts, so we create our reality according to the quality and conditioning of our thoughts. This means that if we train ourselves to be observant of our thoughts, good or bad, little by little we will be able to integrate the totality of our experience with the Akashic Records into our lives. Being able to have this integration, regardless of the information we receive, will allow us to transcend sadness and pain. We will be able to slowly start separating from Samsara and move to a state of balance and a life of joy, service, love, and devotion. Your life will be a well-planned adventure. We know that every adventure has a certain amount of risk, but the risk is worth taking because the rewards of the journey cannot be replaced. These rewards are the gems that we collect from the adventure; and in doing so, we develop an appetite for life. It is as though a new aliveness takes over, and we lose control of the life of self. We surrender to the guidance we receive from the Akashic Records, and we maintain balance and equilibrium in our lives.

On the road of Action and self-discovery, you have the Akashic Records as a tool to guide you through and around obstacles. However, you also need to be aware of the mental patterns you have developed. One such pattern is personal sabotage, and it will constantly remind you that *this is not for you*, or *it is too hard* or *it's taking too long*. It may remind you that there are other tools out there, and maybe you need to go to the spiritual supermarket again and find the next best thing. This is your ego talking, the one that will encourage you to do something while asserting that it *just won't work*. This is the one that constantly whispers in your ear that you are not worthy, that you don't have the right education, the right accent, personality, money. Who is creating all of these thoughts? If you guessed the mind, you are absolutely right. If you have fallen into this trap yourself (and who hasn't?), it is as though you've been creating too many hopes and awakening too many fears. You will be creating a lot of "mental gossip" and, with it, a fallback. (A fallback occurs when the mind takes over and starts judging and criticizing, essentially *falling back* into past experiences that are not supportive of what we are creating at the present moment.) When the mind falls back or regresses to the past and identifies with previous failures or with a program that we have inherited from others, doubts and fears creep up, which in turn cause us to take several steps back or to abandon hope altogether.

This is why the View is so important. Through the dialogue you create with the Masters, you will be able to keep your mind—the ego—in check. They will give you x-ray vision and the ability to zoom into specifics about the past, including past lives, as well as the present. In doing so, they will help guide you into Action. Don't assume that the path of self-discovery is easy, or that getting to the point of truly knowing yourself will happen as fast as turning a light switch on in a darkened room. Understanding the nature of the mind and cultivating a meaningful relationship with the Masters takes dedication and time. But take heart: Developing this relationship will enable you to navigate the vast ocean of Samsara on a well-built boat and with expert navigation at hand.

Many people assume that because they understand something intellectually, they have actually realized it. This is not the case. It takes maturity, time, dedication, observation, meditation, and a sustained relationship with Akasha to be able to realize what one knows. This assumption can be one of the greatest traps set up by the altered ego. Take this as a question to the Akashic

Records and to Meditation. See what parts of you, which of the many masks that you wear during the day (the mask at the office, at home, at a party, at church, when you are talking with your friends, and so on) are attached to what you know. When in conversation, you will defend what you know with all your might, but knowing something intellectually cannot and will not give you self-realization.

Even the greatest Masters have felt the joys and sorrows of life; there are many examples of individuals like this. The difference between an ordinary person and a Master is that the ordinary person is not willing to explore his emotions; instead, he just goes through the motions of life. An ordinary person will instinctively accept or reject his feelings, and this attachment or that aversion will result in a constant accumulation of emotions that are not transmuted, which yields negative karma. On the other hand, the Master, the self-realized individual, is the one who perceives everything that rises in its natural, pristine state without allowing grasping and attachment to enter his perception. This individual views his emotions and reacts to them from a conscious space.

If you are following the thread here, you can clearly see that all of these are part of Action, but they are also a part of the View and Meditation. It is all a part of your Akashic Records. Parts of those Records are stored in your mind. It is all about the mind and what we store there, about being willing to look deep within without getting frustrated. It is about making a commitment to keep on going no matter what because, ultimately, it is worth it. Study this material with the beginner's mind. The beginner's mind is empty, open, and receptive. The expert mind is full. The expert mind knows it all. It is the one that will say, "I know all of this already"; the ego is attached to it. If you come into a situation from the stance of the expert mind, you allow very little to come in.

I have mentioned clinging and attachments before, so let me clarify the difference between attachment and non-attachment. Imagine walking through a beautiful garden. You are completely aware of the beauty and splendor around you. You are aware of the vibrant colors of the flowers and trees, of the temperature, and of the color of the sky. You are aware of how the ground feels as you walk, how the soft grass allows your feet to sink and rebound a bit as you move over it. You are able to perceive the shapes of everything around you, down to minute details, and the scents are almost intoxicating. As you walk around in admiration of the place, there is no trace of clinging or attachment. You leave the place fulfilled, but not in need of *owning* it. In a way, you leave the place even more beautiful than you were before because you are not taking or destroying. What you leave behind are your love and appreciation for what you have seen and enjoyed. Attachment, on the other hand, is like walking through the same beautiful garden and wanting to own it, plucking the flowers, taking some of the stones and crystals for yourself. In other words, you don't leave it in as beautiful a state as it was because you take from it. You leave it with less so you can have more.

The more you cultivate the energy of non-attachment, the more you will gain confidence and serenity that only grows inward as the result of walking through many gardens like this one in awe and admiration, rather than ownership. This will leave a peaceful smile of satisfaction on your face, a sense of humor will arise, and life will be far more pleasurable than ever before.

15

Protection

When we eventually review the Sacred Prayer, you will see that once you are in your Records, you will receive the protection from the Masters and Teachers. You will be receiving a shield of love and light that will protect you energetically from any negative forces that may try to get to you because you are emanating high amounts of inner light.

Spiritual protection is something that everyone should know how to do, regardless of one's religious beliefs. Most people who follow a spiritual path recognize the need for protection from external forces, which encompass far more than just ghosts, entities, and spirits (although if you are a dedicated lightworker, entities are a major force looking to diminish your light). Entities manifest in many forms, but for the most part they are attached to addictions; so there are entities associated with tobacco, alcohol, various drugs, gambling, sex, food, shopping, porn, you name it.

I hold my annual Akashic Records Intensive in Bali. It is one of my favorite places in the world, and the locals have a beautiful ritual. They make small baskets of offerings every day. They make two identical baskets with flowers, cookies, a candy or two, rice, and a stick of incense. One of the baskets is for an altar inside their home or business and is dedicated to the gods. The second basket is left on the floor outside the front door of their home, office, or business; this one is for the demons, ghosts, and entities. They know that demons exist so they might as well satisfy their needs, feeding them outside of the home so they don't come inside to disturb the occupants. In this way, while the demons are outside feasting, the gods and benevolent spirits can come inside the house.

What these entities want from you is to continue in your addiction so they can take in your light and give it to the larger entity to which they are attached. In other words, if you are addicted to nicotine, every time you take a puff, you are losing a certain amount of your light and giving it to the entity. This entity, in turn, gives it to a much larger entity—let's call it the mother nicotine entity—which, fed with this global energy, is able to grow and keep millions of people powerfully addicted. In maintaining your addiction, you not only contribute to losing your own light and health but also contribute to the global addiction. The planet suffers from your negative contribution, as well. This is true for any entity attachment. All other addictions make you lose your light and contribute to the diminishing of the light of the planet.

Negativity in any form can be damaging to your energy. The more you engage in negative patterns, the more you are going to "leak" energy and light. Everything that you create is processed first by your mind, so any negativity that emanates from you or that you express to others, is owned by you. Even though sometimes we create the negativity to simply send it to others, it first has to pass through us. Therefore fear, anger, depression, negative people, negative places, arguments, jealousy, greed, and all other negative energies actually create a negative layer around us that is very much like a dark and dingy coat of paint. The more you engage in that negativity, the more coats of paint you layer upon your energy field. As you continue doing this, the negative energy starts leaking all over your life, creating problems at home, at work, and with people you love. For this reason, spiritual cleansings are very important for your person, your home, and your office. I suggest you do this regularly, especially if you are engaged in the work of the Akashic Records and are clearing lots of old material. It is also important when you notice that the energy inside your auric field is not harmonious and your chakras are out of balance. I will explain more about chakras in Chapter 19.

As I mentioned previously, the Akashic Records prayer carries the protection of the Master and Teachers, and this protection works very much like the coat of paint that I mentioned before but in a different way. When you open your Akashic Records once, it is like applying a thin layer of protection. When you open your Records daily for a month, you now have added a thicker protective layer around you. If you open your Records regularly for a year or two, the layer of protection becomes thicker, stronger, and that much more permanent. Remember, we are working with energy, and energy is like a vapor that will dissipate if it is not properly harnessed. The bottom line is, if you are a lightworker, if you have a spiritual practice, you must protect yourself every single day. I suggest you protect yourself every morning as you get ready to start your day. In the same way that you prepare yourself for the activities of your day by taking a shower, getting dressed, and brushing your teeth, you should apply protection as part of your daily routine.

BUBBLE OF LIGHT PROTECTION

The bubble of light protection technique is very simple to do and is very effective. To do this, imagine a sphere, egg, or bubble big enough for you to fit inside. The strength of the egg shape in particular is quite amazing; it is no wonder that nature chose it! Once you have the shape visualized with yourself inside of it, imagine that the walls are about 12 inches thick and made out of unbreakable glass. If you'd like, you can add your own daily prayer to this visualization. Mine is: *I invoke the Light of the Christ within. I am a clear and perfect channel. Light is my guide.*

The inside of the bubble is very important. I'm sure you've experienced the ways in which colors impact your life and your mood. The same applies to the color you put inside the bubble or egg. If you want general protection, use pure white light. Envision it as big and as bright as you can in your mind's eye, feeling it and allowing it to grow as large as you can make it. Once you have the visual or the feeling of it, imagine that you are blowing this white light into your bubble, the same way that you would blow air into a balloon. Do this until you feel it is completely full. This means that you have generated this light within you first; and when you are full, you can fill the bubble.

Here is a list of colors that you can add to the inside of your bubble or egg, depending on the situation that you are going to encounter:

- ↬ Blue: for protection, communication, and flow
- ↬ Green: for giving and receiving healing, balance, and new growth
- ↬ Red: for action and vitality on the physical plane
- ↬ Orange: for procreation, co-creation, and sexuality
- ↬ Yellow: for mental clarity, direction, and focus
- ↬ Purple: for spirituality and wisdom

- White: for purity, connection, and enlightenment
- Peach: for flattery (it brings out the best in everything and everyone!)
- Pink: for sweetness and humility
- Turquoise: for self-worth and as a purifier
- Pearlescent: contains all colors and is good for everything
- Silver: for attention and flow, and to be noticed
- Gold: for Christ consciousness
- Gray: for intensity or to intensify your actions
- Brown: for grounding and stabilization
- Black : for containing, absorbing, and consuming

This is a wonderful list of colors that you can add to the inside of your bubble or egg. There will also be times when you have to do something to the outside of the bubble, depending on the circumstances in your life. If you are experiencing a psychic attack, receiving negativity and waves of anger, jealousy, or criticism

Diagram 5. The bubble of light protection technique.

from a source known or unknown, you may want to coat the outside of the bubble with a reflecting surface like a mirror. You may be asking why you would want to do this. First of all, and most importantly, you are not responsible for the projections or energy of others. By reflecting the energy back to the source, you give that individual the opportunity to take ownership of his or her projections. They are not for you to deal with; you have enough of your own stuff! The most important thing is to always reflect back with love and compassion. Do it knowing that what you ultimately want is the highest good for all concerned.

THREE-LAYER PROTECTION

The three-layer protection is another simple yet effective way to protect yourself. To do this, see yourself standing and gathering all of your energy into your heart. Feel how all your intention funnels into the center of your heart. From this space, generate a feeling of love, and allow that feeling to gently grow and take over your entire body. Feel the temperature of love radiating out of your heart like gentle waves of heat; visualize the color blue, like a flame. Allow that sensation to travel approximately 12 feet in front of your body and there, create a bubble or an egg shape all around you. See it as clearly as you can, and make it thick. See and feel the heat that continues to emanate from your heart, and apply it to the exterior surface of the bubble.

Return your attention to your heart, and once again generate those feelings of love. Feel your heart expanding. This time visualize the color green. Make it the most beautiful green you have ever seen. Allow it to travel approximately 6 feet in front of you, just as before, and create a bubble or egg shape around you. See it as clearly as you can. Coat the bubble with the color green that you generated.

Return your attention to your heart, and again start generating feelings of love and compassion. This time imagine a golden and luminous color, and imagine it generating energy in the center of your chest, your heart chakra. There, see it as a golden, luminescent ball approximately 4 to 5 inches in diameter. Feel it vibrating and moving. Feel and know that the energy within the sphere is alive. Feel it becoming the essence of love and compassion more and more, and feel the electric qualities contained within it.

Allow that ball of energy to gently escape from your heart and travel approximately 3 feet in front of your body, and there create a sphere or an egg shape. Make it as strong as you can and see the golden luminous color radiating all around it.

Now see yourself standing in the center of all three egg-shaped layers. Think of Russian dolls that fit one inside the other. The first egg shape, the one with the heat,

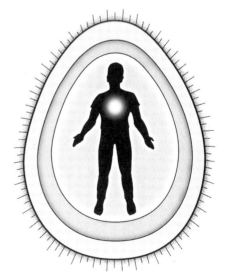

Diagram 6. Three-layer protection.

is going to burn and keep away any energy projected at you from any source known or unknown. It is going to keep you protected from the world at large, especially energies of malintent, negativity, anger, criticism, and envy. The second egg shape, the green one, is going to create a second layer of protection. Here you will allow energy to pass through the first layer and bring it closer to you; here you can store energies of healing either given or received. The third egg shape is the one closest to you. The color is golden, and this layer is your most intimate layer. Here you allow Spirit to enter. This is your most intimate space, a space of inner meditation and communion with the self. This is the space that is reserved for your most intimate relationships, inner exploration, prayer, celebration, and love.

CLEARING YOUR HOME OR OFFICE OF NEGATIVE ENERGY

Regular spiritual house clearings are important to remove any negative energy that's lingering around. Everything in your home, from carpets, furniture, and pictures to appliances and even wall paint, can become caked with energy. Every negative event or outburst (such as an episode of sarcasm, anger, rage, or abuse) will leave an energetic imprint in your home. If you do nothing about it, you'll essentially be allowing negativity to accumulate in your home. If you move to a new home or office, you really don't know what went on there before you moved in. Perhaps the former occupants emanated tremendous amounts of anger and dissatisfaction. Perhaps there was arguing, crying, or even violence to the point that someone was hurt or even killed. You just never know. No matter what, it is always best to do a complete house clearing.

Before we start, let me be very clear about this procedure. *It involves fire, and you have to be extremely careful when you do it.* You don't want to take any risks of injuring or burning yourself or your property.

This is a twofold ritual. The first part is to remove, let go of, and extract everything negative from the house. Everything, good and bad, leaves. The second part is to invite and welcome the spirits that you want. By spirits, I mean saints, Christ, Buddha, angels, archangels, and so on. I do not mean the spirits of deceased people.

This is what you will need:

- ↫ One large frying pan
- ↫ Aluminum foil

- Epsom salts
- Alcohol
- A pot holder
- White sage and a bowl in which to burn it
- A lighter with a long nozzle to prevent you from burning your hand

Note: This is going to produce a very strong fire so be very cautious. Have someone with you in case you need support holding the frying pan. Use pot holders, not towels, to hold the frying pan because it will get very hot. **Do not do this near curtains, dried flowers, or anything else that can catch fire easily. And do not do this if you don't feel comfortable with fire.** You may want to start the process with a very small amount of Epsom salts and alcohol and see how you feel.

Start by having a clean home, making it as uncluttered as possible, especially in the corners. Sweep or vacuum the floors, removing all dust and dirt. This is an important step—don't skip it! Then, create an energy of protection around you. Ask your angels, spirit guides, gods, and goddesses to protect you. You can also open your Akashic Records, as this will make the ritual more powerful. Remind yourself that what you are doing is for the highest good of everyone concerned. You can use the same prayer I gave you previously as you walk around the house, repeating constantly:

I invoke the Light of the Christ within. I am a clear and perfect channel. Light is my guide.

1. Line the frying pan with the aluminum foil. Add Epsom salts to cover the bottom of the pan (about 1/4 inch deep). Add alcohol to cover the Epsom salts, making sure the alcohol is at least 1/8 inch above the salts.

2. Make sure all windows and doors are open, if possible. This is important because you want to give all the energy, spirits, and entities an easy exit out of the house. Closed doors and windows will keep them trapped.

3. Light the mixture and walk around the room or house. It will produce an intense flame so be *very careful*. Hold the frying pan at arm's length and away from your face. There will be areas where the fire will get angry. Stop there for a moment until it slows down a bit. These are areas of accumulated energy, and they need to be released and consumed by the fire.

4. Walk from corner to corner of the room to clear every inch of the space, and then move to the next room. When finished, place the frying pan on a potholder, a tile, a trivet, or a cement floor. The bottom is going to be extremely hot and it will burn anything that's not heatproof.

5. Once you have completed this part, close all windows and doors. This way, all the energies you want to bring into the house, through your invocations and prayer, will stay in the house. Call for the Light and invite the saints, Buddha's, bodhisattvas, or benevolent spirits you work with.

The next part of the process is done with white sage or another sacred herb such as sweetgrass, copal, or frankincense. You can also use incense if you don't have white sage. Make sure all fire alarms are disabled because of the smoke.

1. Start at the same place as before. Light the sage and then blow out the flame so the sage can produce smoke. Slowly walk from corner to corner of each room as you did before.

2. Use the prayer or mantra of your choice to invite the good spirits and call in the angels. Visualize peace, love, and harmony, and feel the energy that you want to protect your home. Play beautiful devotional music to fill the space.

3. Tie a white sage flower above the entrance or entrances of your home. This will keep your home protected.

4. Light a candle, place it on your altar, and give thanks and gratitude for all that you have learned and done.

There is another way that you can clear your home, but it is not meant to replace the previous recipe. Dilute pure salt, rock salt, or unrefined sea salt with purified water and put it in a spray bottle. Walk around each room from corner to corner, spaying the water. This acts as a neutralizer.

SMUDGING

Smudging is a beautiful ceremony. I was introduced to it in Mexico when I was a child, not knowing what the shamans or medicine men or women were doing as I watched them blow smoke all over the person they were healing or in the home they were cleansing. As I grew older, I learned that they used sacred herbs, including tobacco, to lift or cleanse any negativity from the person or the home. Most native cultures from all over the world have a smudging ritual as part of their traditions.

When I started attending sweat lodges here in the United States more than 20 years ago, my spiritual grandmother (although she always called me brother, so we finally settled on "grandsis") talked about smudging. Her name is Barrett Eagle Bear, and she is a medicine woman from the Lakota tradition. She always said that negative spirits cannot stand to be in the presence or the scent of sage but that positive spirits are attracted to its scent. To me, smudging is akin to a spiritual vacuum cleaner. Anything that is caked inside your auric field is going to be removed. Any energy that lingers after a healing session or an episode of anger can and should be cleared with this method.

You can use any sacred herb such as white sage, sweet grass, copal, frankincense, myrrh, or pure tobacco (not for smoking) to remove negativity. I use loose white sage. I place some of it in a ceramic bowl and light it. As the sage is smoking, the person whom you are smudging stands with legs and arms spread apart. Starting from the top, you fan the smoke from head to toe, passing the bowl over and around the arms and legs. Once you do the front, move to the back and do the same thing so that both front and back are covered. If you have a smudging fan, even better. This way you don't have to use your hand or blow it with your breath. It is also more traditional.

HOW WILL I KNOW IF I AM PROTECTED OR NOT?

Being unprotected normally manifests itself within the emotional and spiritual bodies. Following is a list of symptoms you may experience if your energy field is unprotected:

- Feeling irritable, short-tempered, and impatient with people
- Feeling drained
- Experiencing nightmares
- Being easily influenced by others
- Feeling threatened/defensive
- Becoming fanatical about someone
- Feeling other people's emotions or pain
- Bumping into people and things
- Copying or living your life through others
- Feeling physical pain in the back of your neck, solar plexus (pit of the stomach), or joints

You can build up and protect your energy field in a number of ways. Here are a few easy steps to follow:

- Open your Akashic Records daily.
- Create your bubble of protection daily.
- Keep fit and physically healthy.
- Drink plenty of water.
- Wear protective colors or colors that make you feel good.
- Wear or carry crystals with protective qualities—for example, amethyst, lapis lazuli, sugilite, larimar, gold tiger's eye, and hawk's eye (blue tiger's eye)—for psychic protection.
- Wear or use protective symbols. (Symbols are very personal and will depend on your beliefs, so use whatever feels right and helpful to you.)

16

Grounding

Grounding is a significant foundation upon which many other practices are built. It just stands to reason that if you are not grounded and solidly planted on this earth, you are going to be shaky and vulnerable. I imagine many of you have heard of grounding or have practiced it in some way. It is a simple but important step that should not be missed. Grounding is the act of consciously creating an energy connection from your body into the earth. Grounding helps keep the energy body strong and prevents it from becoming overly stressed. It helps to keep your energy system safe when you are doing spiritual work or when you prepare to open your Akashic Records. Grounding will align you with the core of the earth; this, in itself, will also align your chakras. Grounding acts in the same way as an electrical ground that keeps you from getting electrocuted. We already know that your energy increases as a result of spending time in the Akashic Records, so you can see why this would be necessary.

Maybe you have experienced the feeling of not being grounded. Perhaps you have attended a ritual or given or received a strong healing session, and afterward felt slightly nauseous, had a headache, or felt "spacey." In many cases, this is the natural reaction of the body to more intense energy moving through it when it does not have the capacity to house the energy being received. Think about grounding as a way to assist you in either holding onto the energy being received or releasing un-needed energy. When you ground yourself, you release unwanted or excess energy and it gets transformed by mother earth. It becomes part of the earth's natural recycling process.

Grounding can also help you release someone else's energy that you have taken on for some reason. This happens many times during healing sessions when the person being healed dumps a bunch of energy and the healer is not aware of what is taking place. This energy is cumulative; if you don't release it, and if you don't ground yourself afterward, little by little it will start affecting you. If it does, you will start feeling tired, unusual body aches and pains will start coming up, and you will feel emotional and depleted.

THE IMPORTANCE OF BEING GROUNDED

Here are a few ways that being grounded can make a big difference in your everyday life:

- Allows for our deep connection between heaven and earth, giving us a greater ability to be balanced

- Increases our healing abilities by pulling sacred energies from the earth

- Gives us the opportunity to maintain equilibrium between our physical, mental, and emotional bodies

- Helps us to remain fully connected to the earth and life itself, and helps us realize we are here to fulfill a purpose

- Helps to maintain a flow between spirit and matter

- Provides the means to release blocked, untransmuted energy more easily

- Allows us to grow deeper roots, and with that, the possibility of higher spiritual attainment

After spending long periods of time in the Akashic Records energy, you can become ungrounded. If you have a healing practice of any kind, whether you are a psychotherapist, a massage therapist, or a Reiki practitioner, and you keep your Akashic Records open during the sessions, you might feel a little ungrounded at the end because of the exchange of energy. It is extremely important to stop what you're doing and take care of yourself. After all, you are the vessel, the vehicle, which must remain balanced and strong to help others.

Here are steps you can take to stay grounded:

- ↪ Take a walk barefoot on the earth and visualize energy flowing down toward your feet and out to the earth.
- ↪ Go to the park, your yard, or the forest and hug a tree. Give it all of your energy and let it take it and transmute it for you.
- ↪ Eat anything that grows underground: potatoes, carrots, beets, turnips, rutabagas, onions, sweet potatoes, and so on.
- ↪ Drink plenty of water with a high pH.
- ↪ Walk in natural surroundings. Walk on the earth rather than pavement.
- ↪ Do physical exercise: sports, yoga, tai chi, dance, etc.
- ↪ Work with your hands in the earth. Plant flowers and cultivate a garden.
- ↪ Find your purpose in life and follow it.
- ↪ Visualize roots coming out of your feet and deeply anchoring you in the earth.
- ↪ Carry or wear grounding crystals such as black tourmaline, onyx, hematite, black obsidian, smoky quartz, or bloodstone.
- ↪ Engage in grounding visualization and meditation, which I will share with you in the following section.

GROUNDING VISUALIZATION

Start with your feet flat on the ground. I have already mentioned that you can visualize a tree with deep roots. Imagine you have deep roots coming from the bottoms of your feet. If you are sitting, you can visualize these roots coming from the base of your spine, down your legs, and all the way to the floor. Simply allow these roots to go deep down and anchor you to the earth. Feel the electromagnetic pull of the core of the earth. At the same time, feel your crown chakra being pulled straight up to the heavens, creating a solid and strong line of energy between heaven and earth.

GROUNDING MEDITATION

I suggest you record this meditation so you don't have to read it. This will make your experience much more powerful. Or, even easier, go to my Website (*www.journeytotheheart.com*) and download it for free under Free Stuff.

Sit comfortably in a straight-back chair or on the floor on a cushion. Have your hands and feet apart and feet flat on the floor. Close your eyes (this helps you to focus internally). Take three deep breaths. Breathe down into your belly and "soften" your belly as you breathe. Allow your abdomen to expand and naturally contract. Breathe through your nose while keeping your tongue resting lightly on the roof of your mouth. Be mindful and aware as you breathe. Notice how your body naturally relaxes. Simply feel and be present.

Be aware of your first chakra. This is the energy center that is closest to the earth, located at the base of the spine. The color of this energy center is red. Generate energy to this area by bringing your attention there. Allow the sensations and feelings to gently flow down toward your feet. Let this energy flow down through the floor, down through the building where you are, and down to connect with the earth. Let this energy gently flow down and down until it connects with the heart of the mother, until it reaches the center, the core of the earth. Feel the magnetic pull of the earth. Feel its gravity and feel the deep pull of your first chakra.

Once you feel grounded, relax and gently breathe; experience your grounding and feel your connection to Mother Earth, Pachamama. Feel your spiritual connection with this beautiful planet. Notice how your body feels, grounding and becoming more present. Be in the moment; release any tension or physical discomfort; gently breathe in through your nose and out your mouth; and allow the energy to flow.

Now gently visualize a waterfall with cool, beautiful, refreshing water, and see how it is cascading from the base of your spine down through your legs. See how it nourishes and refreshes as it connects and flows with all reality. It's flowing and flowing without resistance, down through your roots to the center of the earth, to the heart of the mother. Know the waters that flow from you are connected to your emotions and offer this to her. Experience this with an open heart. Experience the bliss and simply relax. Stay like this as long as you want. Take your time.

Now gently change your visualization and see the beautiful and strong roots of a tree, allowing them to grow slowly and strongly. See them going down all the way to the center of the earth, to connect and embrace the heart of the mother. Notice how this changes your experience. Breathe, enjoy, and take your time.

Now, connecting with your feelings and emotions, breathe into your first chakra and create, imagine, visualize on your own. Create your own grounding. What do you see? How does it feel? Be playful, take your time, and breathe. Release physical, emotional, and mental tension, body aches and pains, and memories from past experiences, or simply the unwanted energy from your last session. Let it all gently flow out of your body into the earth. Take your time and notice how you feel as you do this, as you empty out. Go deep within. Be still, and relax. Be open, and listen.

When you are done, slowly open your eyes, take a deep breath, stretch your arms over your head, and exhale with a sigh as if you were waking up in the morning. Bend forward and touch your hands to the ground. Give thanks to Mother Earth for the support that she gives you, for the nourishment and the life you have. Give her thanks for being the body that is strong enough to ground you and sustain you. Bring your hands together and say aloud, "Thank you!"

17

Akashic Records Consultation Guidelines

Here are eight important guidelines to keep in mind as you work with the Akashic Records.

1. WORK WITH A FULLY CONSCIOUS MIND. KEEP CLOSED EYES TO A MINIMUM TO AVOID TRANCE CHANNELING. BE AWARE OF YOUR ENVIRONMENT WHEN YOU OPEN YOUR RECORDS.

We keep our eyes open so we don't fall into a space where we lose awareness and go into trance. In this system of the Akashic Records, you don't need special talents or psychic abilities. If you have them, set them aside, and give yourself permission to learn this method intact and as pure as it is. Once you have learned it and developed a relationship with the Lords of Akasha, then ask how to best introduce your special talents and abilities and use them in conjunction with the Akashic Records. The only requirement that you need in order to successfully open your Akashic Records is an open heart.

The Akashic Records are about being conscious and aware, not unconscious. In most of my classes I ask my students, "How many of you are meditators or practice meditation regularly?" I would say that a good 85 to 90 percent raise their hands. Then I ask, "What happens when you first close your eyes and take a deep breath? Where do you go?" I ask them to try it and feel it. Try it now. Put the book down, close your eyes, take a deep breath, and see where you go. After you exhale, stay in that space for about 10 seconds and then open your eyes. Where did you go?

The answers are always similar: some place deep within, to the silence, to a void, to a space of inner peace, and so on. No one ever tells me they felt completely aware of their surroundings. One of the goals of meditation is to push you deep within, but with the Akashic Records, we want to remain fully conscious and aware. That is why we keep eye closing to a minimum. Keeping your eyes closed for a long time when you are sitting to receive information from the Masters can create a pattern of interference.

2. Do not drive a car or use heavy equipment or machinery with your Akashic Records open.

We enter an altered state of consciousness while in the Records. Once you open them, you will experience a shift. For some people, it is dramatic and noticeable; for others, it is more subtle. Either way is perfect. However, there is a shift, and if you start receiving a big download of information while in this space, it is not safe for you to be driving or operating machinery.

3. The Akashic Records prayer is sacred. Protect it and carry it with you at all times. If making personal copies, do not copy the directions for its use. This protects the prayer if it is misplaced.

A long time ago, I typed the Sacred Prayer on a business card. I had the Sacred Prayer on one side and the four other prayers on the other. That way, wherever I am in the world, I have the prayers with me in my pocket. You may want to laminate the card. Knowing that the prayer is sacred and that the Akashic Records are not for everyone—not yet, anyway—you'll want to protect it at all times. At the same time, you'll want to have it with you because you just never know when you are going to need it.

4. No recreational drugs or excessive drinking 24 hours before you open your Akashic Records. Prescription medications are acceptable, however.

The reason for this should be obvious: You don't want to alter your consciousness. You want to be as clear as you can so that you can receive clear messages. You shouldn't open your Records when you are tipsy, as it can create a pattern of interference.

5. Use your first and last legal name to open your Akashic Records.

This is important because of the vibrational frequency of your name. Over the years, we have all created a frequency or magnetic resonance with our name, and the Akashic Records will open to that vibrational frequency.

If you have recently gotten married and have taken the last name of your husband, you may want to use your maiden name. If you have changed your name to a New Age name, or if a guru changed your name for you, and you have not embodied the vibrational frequency of your new name, you will most likely experience difficulty in getting information. It can create a pattern of interference. If this is the case, open your Records with your legal name. However, if you have been using a given name for three to four years, you have integrated that name into your being and will be able to use it without any problems.

Another scenario may occur for some women. Let's say you may have been married some time, but your marriage is not going well and you are considering separation or divorce. The last name of your husband is going to be rejected by your subconscious because you are in conflict with that original energy in real life. In a case like this, open your Records with your maiden name. The best advice I can give you is to simply try it out with all of your possible names. I have had numerous people in my classes with New Age names who receive beautiful information with that new name because it is more real in terms of vibration than the one given to them without a choice. Try it different ways and see what works.

6. ALWAYS READ THE SACRED PRAYER. DO NOT RECITE IT FROM MEMORY.

This is very important. The prayer was given to us in a special way and it comes from the Maya tradition. The way it was written is the way you will receive it in this book. I have not altered it in any way. Keeping the integrity of the original prayer is very important because it has the flow of the original energy. The prayer is alive, and the words are encoded in Sacred Geometry. If you change one word, it changes the whole vibration of the prayer, and you will probably not end up in Akasha when you read it. When you read the prayer correctly, the energetic vibration that entered Johnny Prochaska's crown chakra when the high priest pushed in the prayer is the same energetic vibration that will enter yours. Then it will descend into your heart.

I'll share a personal story about this so you can understand the importance of not changing a single word. A few years ago when I first launched my Website, *www.journeytotheheart.com*, I wanted to let my close friends know that it was ready and have them take a look, so I sent a personal e-mail making the announcement. Shortly after sending the e-mail, I started receiving messages from my friends asking me, "Ernesto, what did you get into? What is this about?" In one of the e-mails, a good friend said to me "Ernesto you wrote *journey to the heat* and not *journey to the heart.*" I laughed out loud and replied to my friends, "I was so hot to get you this information that I sent you to the *heat* instead of the *heart!*" (The funny thing was that the other site was a soft porn Website!)

I love this story, and I am so glad it happened to me because it is the perfect example of the importance of not changing even one letter of the prayer. If you do, the whole vibration will shift, and you will likely end up in a land of imposters. You may get directed to the astral plane or elsewhere. You will not get on the elevator I described that takes you directly from the ground floor to the penthouse; you may end up on another floor altogether. The point is that if you really want to stay in the vibration of the Masters and Teachers, if you really want to develop a relationship with the Sacred Prayer and Akasha, then do not change a single letter or word of the prayer. It was given as a beautiful dispensation from Spirit at a time when we, the world, needed (and still need) this energy the most, so let's keep that integrity and vibration. Bring your energy up to the next level of your own vibratory frequency, which is what this book is all about. Ask yourself the question, *As I increase my vibration, my light, what will be my contribution to humanity and the world?*

We have just recently ended a cosmic cycle; and where there is an end, there is always a new beginning. You are the architect of your own future, and the Akashic Records are here to help you map this out in the best way possible. With your increased vibration and your continued learning of the language of the heart, you can get together with others around the world with similar vibration and consciousness to impact the electromagnetic fields of the earth. As we do this, we can contribute to a positive change in the hearts and minds of people, as well as the planet as a whole. There is no better time to be alive! You have picked the perfect time and place to take embodiment. If you wanted excitement, you are sure to get it. You will be able to witness amazing changes in your life and the world, so get ready for it. As you let go of the past, you are becoming the architect of your future.

7. EXTENDED PERIODS OF TIME IN THE AKASHIC RECORDS ARE NOT RECOMMENDED IN THE BEGINNING.

The Akashic Records create a shift that produces a slightly altered state of consciousness, so it is best to start slowly and gradually increase the time you spend in the Records. As you continue reading, you will see the simplicity of opening your Records; you can open them four to five times a day with ease. I often compare the Akashic Records to a muscle like your biceps. If you have never worked out with weights before and you try to curl a 50-pound weight, you probably won't be able to do it. You might even injure yourself. The muscle is not trained and cannot handle it. You have to start with a five-pound weight and go slowly. Little by little, you gain strength until you can move up to a 15-pound weight, and so on until you graduate up to 50 pounds. In the same manner, little by little, you start increasing the amount of time you spend in the Records' energy. At first you should remain for no more than 15 minutes. Gradually, you'll increase your time to 30 minutes, and then an hour or two, until you are very comfortable with the energy.

Sometimes students ask me if it is okay to have their Akashic Records open all day, and my reply is always, "For what purpose?" If the Records are sacred, then they should be treated with respect. It is similar to owning something precious and valuable, something you keep locked in a safe or in a cabinet behind glass. Would you walk around all day long with that something in your hands, as you do all the mundane things that you have to do like pumping gas, going to the grocery store, shopping, or going to the post office? You wouldn't. You would be afraid that something so precious would fall and break or be lost or stolen. However, you bring it out at home because it is safe and contained. It is the same with the Akashic Records and the energy and service the Masters provide for you. Respect it; use it; get guidance and inspiration from it; and then put it away. Don't waste the energy of the Masters by keeping your Records open all day. Continue using your free will and make the right choices as you go through all the mundane stuff.

8. EXPLORE A FEW SUBJECT AREAS FOR FORMULATING QUESTIONS.

Your experience with the Akashic Records is uniquely your own. Learning to formulate questions is an art. This is one of the most valuable tools for exploring the Records and deriving information. If you ask a yes-or-no question, you will receive a yes-or-no answer. Know that the Record Keepers will answer the question you ask as you have asked it, no more and no less.

If there is something that you don't understand, ask for clarification. Ask for it to be explained to you in a different way. You can also try asking sub-questions so you can get deeper into the subject matter until you are clear and satisfied. Ask and you will receive.

Here is a list of areas you may want to consider exploring with the Akashic Records. Later on, I will give you more specific questions.

- Current life challenges and circumstances
- Interactions with friends and family
- Repeated patterns and behaviors
- Reoccurring dreams
- Influences from past lives
- Spiritual growth or path
- Life purpose and direction
- Influences from outside sources
- Patterns of addiction and codependency
- Contracts created in this or previous lifetimes
- Familial, romantic, and professional relationships
- Spiritual path and direction

18

The Akashic Records Sacred Prayer and Opening Your Records

When you open your Akashic Records with the Sacred Prayer, you align yourself with the vibration of your own Book of Life. The prayer works with energetic vibrations to key in to the specific name of the person and carries with it the protection of the Masters and Teachers. To open your Akashic Records you must use your name to create the right vibration or frequency. This is very important. As I already mentioned, you want to use your first and last legal name, the name that is on your birth certificate. If you are a woman and have taken the last name of your husband, it is perfectly okay to use that name as long as you feel that you have integrated the energy of that name into your life. If you are recently married, in the last year or two, and feel you have not yet integrated that last name into your energetic field, you may want to use your maiden name. If you have been married longer but your marriage is not in harmony and you are considering separation or divorce, you may want to use your maiden name.

Another special situation is if a guru has given you a new, spiritual name. Suppose your name was Larry Williams but your new, spiritual name is Jai Ganapati. If this new name is not fully integrated into all aspects of your life, including your four lower bodies—mental, emotional, physical and spiritual—it is best to use your birth name. Every now and then, you can ask the Masters if you are ready to open your Akashic Records with your spiritual name. Do not force the information with an attachment to your new name. If you do this, you may create a pattern of interference.

In this chapter we are finally going to explore the Akashic Records Prayer itself. I will give you the Sacred Prayer intact, as I received it, as Mary received it, and as Johnny Prochaska received it at the beginning. (For more on the story of how Johnny received the prayer, see Appendix A. It's a fascinating story in its own right!) The most important thing about the Akashic Records is the Sacred Prayer; again, the one thing that we *do not do* is change the wording of the prayer. We keep it intact, exactly as it was received by Johnny, which is the way it is presented here, in this book. The prayer was given to us in Mayan, from which it was translated into Spanish, English, and then into many different languages, but always keeping the integrity of the wording.

After the prayer, I will explain it line by line, so you have a complete and full understanding of it. I will also explain what I call the "AAA recipe" and its importance in opening your Records. As I mentioned before, there is a formula for opening your Records. Simply reading the prayer as it is written will not yield anything. The formula must be followed in order to fully activate the energy between you and Akasha.

The formula for opening your Akashic Records:

1. Do your centering exercise and the AAA recipe (see page 132 at the end of this chapter), and bring all of your attention to your heart.

2. Read the Akashic Records Sacred Prayer out loud, exactly as it is written, *once*.

3. Repeat the prayer *two times in silence*, replacing the word *me* with your first and last name.

Be open to receive the energy. Feel the shift as the energy gently descends to your crown chakra, like a waterfall or liquid light entering your crown and slowly bathing your entire body. Sit in the energy and receive. There are different ways of receiving the information based on the degree to which your senses are developed. I will discuss this in greater depth later.

To open your Records, repeat the following Sacred Prayer:

*"I ask God if He will have His Shield of Love and Truth around **me** permanently, so only God's Love and Truth will exist between you and me."*

*"I allow the Masters, Teachers, and Loved Ones of **me** to channel through me, out of whatever realm, to say whatever they wish."*

To close your Records, repeat the following:

"I thank the Masters, Teachers, and Loved Ones for the information they have given me today. I trust that this information has been given for my highest good. Amen."

The first part of the prayer reads, *I ask God if He will have His Shield of Love and Truth around me permanently.* This refers to the shield of protection I mentioned earlier in the book. You will have this shield of protection when you are enhanced by the energy of the Records. Remember, the more you develop a relationship with the Records, the stronger the protection will become. It is no different than building a muscle or adding coats of paint to a wall. Little by little, the energy builds up, and it will linger long after you close your Akashic Records.

Sometimes during my classes, someone complains about the use of the word *he* or *his*, which you see twice in the prayer. The Masters have shared with me that in the eyes of Spirit, there is no division or distinction between male and female, between he and she. There is equality at the soul level, and gender is irrelevant. They have also told me that when this prayer was actively used during the time of the Mayas, there was gender equality so there were no issues regarding gender. Enter the words and the sacred space that the prayer will create for you with complete equality and with no sense of gender or separation.

The second part of the paragraph reads *so only God's Love and Truth will exist between you and me.* Here we are asking for the absolute truth that can come to us from God's grace, the truth that the Masters have to share with us for our illumination and growth. We are asking for the most divine love that can possibly descend from Akasha to envelop us, to surround us, and to protect us. There is nothing more delicious than to sit in the energy of God's love. Now let us understand the last part, *between you and me.* Who are *you* and *me* referring to? *You* in this case refers to the Masters and Teachers, and *me* refers to you, the person opening his or her own Records.

The second portion of the prayer reads, *I allow the Masters, Teachers, and Loved Ones of me....* By now we are clear who the Masters and Teachers are.

"Loved Ones" are people you have known who have made their transition. In most cases, these are close family members that have unfinished karmic business with you. In other words, they are trapped in limbo or in the astral plane, waiting to have this communication with you so that they can have their peace and continue on to their spiritual evolution without any karmic bonds holding them back. It may be you, the one clinging to their memory, who has not allowed them to move to spiritual freedom. If you are clinging to them, it is like putting a chain around their neck; it keeps them bound to the earth plane. They have come to ask you to let them go. It is possible that someone other than a family member can come through to ask you for assistance in being released to the light. This situation can occur when the need is there and the energy link is created; many times, this is done without your conscious knowing. The Masters will bring a soul into your presence in order for that soul to have communication and resolution. Another thing that may very well happen is that other souls who have passed on who were once in close proximity to you will know they can come and ask for help because of the inner light you will be emanating. They will come and ask for help so they can move to spiritual liberation and continue to the schools of light.

Please note that this prayer will allow you to access only your own Records. To open the Akashic Records of others, you need to learn a different prayer. Please keep in mind that there are three levels of training for the Akashic Records. This book covers just the first level, accessing your own Records. It is the first and most important step.

Continuing with the prayer, the second part of the paragraph reads, *to channel through me, out of whatever realm, to say whatever they wish.* The phrase *to channel through me* refers to the fact that you will be used as a conduit for information. A channel refers to something that contains a liquid that flows. In this case, you are that channel, and the liquid that flows is the information and the energy given to you by the Masters and Teachers.

Out of whatever realm is important to understand correctly. This does not refer to the realms of the more dense levels of consciousness. It does not come from the astral, mental, or emotional planes. Rather, it refers to a realm within Akasha, any realm within the many different floors and departments of the Library of Congress of the soul. In trusting that you have deeply connected to the Records, the Masters will tell you whatever they wish for your highest good, based on your question. Remember, once your Akashic Records are open, you can merely sit in the energy for overall healing. Or, you can ask the Masters to take you to the Teachers who have the expertise you need and who can tutor you in specific subjects of interest. The possibilities are endless; it is all up to you and your willingness to use your creativity and imagination.

At the end of the time you spend in the Akashic Records, you will want to close your Records. Say to yourself or aloud, "I thank the Masters, Teachers, and Loved Ones for the information they have given me today. I trust that this information has been given for my highest good. Amen." This is an acknowledgment, an expression of your gratitude, for what you have received.

What the sacred prayer does:

- Opens a portal, creates a frequency and a shift that promotes healing
- Aligns the chakras
- Brings sacred energies right to the heart
- Expands your auric field
- Gives you greater sensitivity
- Connects you to a sacred source of information
- Gives you direction and inspiration
- Generates pure feelings of love and compassion
- Enhances or brings to the next level any process or endeavor, now or in the future
- Deepens your meditation and personal spiritual practice
- Creates a strong shield of protection
- Gives you the opportunity to heal old patterns
- Gives you a direct line of communication with the Masters and Teachers

Always remember:

- Do a mini centering and grounding meditation.
- Do your AAA recipe (see pages 132).
- Read the Akashic Records prayer so that you do not accidentally transpose the words.

The words of the prayer are alive and encoded; as we receive the energy of the Records, we ourselves become encoded.

Here, finally, is the Akashic Records prayer in Mayan hieroglyphs to give you a visual of how the original prayer might have looked. Bear in mind that the original prayer has been lost, so this is for illustration purposes only.

⊷

THE SACRED PRAYER IN MAYAN

Ichi K'oj K'awil Naka Utom Ch'am u B'ah pakal
B'a Juntan i Juntan i Jaj Ak'e ni Ixin
Nahatir Che'n Tocot K'oj K'awil Juntan i
Jaj Utom Nak K'ub a i ni
Yaj Pasaj u Cha'n B'ah Ajaw i Olas K'uh
Caniyal B'a ni Tac Chich Man'l taanil ni
Awa't ta Ox Hun Tac A'al Ox Jajaa'cic C'atiineeb

⊷

THE AAA RECIPE: THE FORMULA FOR OPENING YOUR AKASHIC RECORDS

The AAA recipe is an essential component of opening the Akashic Records. It is the way we center ourselves and bring sacred energies to the heart. AAA stands for *align, attune,* and *allow.*

Once you are ready to open your Akashic Records, the first step is to create a sacred space. You can do this in whatever way is comfortable for you. You can sit in front of an altar, if you have one, light a candle, burn incense, ground yourself, and so on. It helps to do a mini centering meditation, too. Take a deep breath and gently drop your attention into your heart. Once you have connected with your heart, open your eyes, look down at the floor, and slowly raise your eyes past the horizon. Approximately 30 degrees above the horizon, you will feel a point at which your eyes and your heart connect. There will be a gentle click and a feeling that your eyes and your heart are connected. This is an important step in practicing open-eyed meditation. As you remember, we keep eye closing to a minimum when we are in the Akashic Records.

From this heart-centered space, you do your first A, *align*. Aligning refers to becoming aware of all of your energy. If you have been out and about, you will most likely feel that it is scattered. Consciously start bringing all the energy to your center, as if you were taking all the energy from the outside and passing it through a funnel that is going straight into your heart. Once there, you will feel a sense of connection. It is as if there were a line pulling you straight up. Feel all of your energy gathered and centered in your heart.

Diagram 7. The Sacred Prayer in Mayan hieroglyphs.

The second A is *attune*. Everything you do, whether it is opening your Akashic Records, sitting in meditation, praying, or doing energy work, has a specific frequency. Attune refers to tuning into this specific frequency. Think of it as an old fashioned radio. One of the knobs is the volume and the other is the one you turn to change the station. We feel the frequency of the Akashic Records and start turning the dial to close in on it. There will be a point where it just "clicks," and you will know that you have attuned to the frequency of Akasha.

The third A is *allow*. Allowing simply means that you open yourself up to receive the energy, the flow of information that comes from Akasha, without obstacles or objections. Allowing is closely related to trust, and trust may be one of the issues you are working with. Without trust, allowing will be difficult, so work on it with an open heart and let the Masters guide you.

Trust is a big issue in our society. When we are young we are programmed not to trust. Our parents are constantly telling us not to trust, and rightfully so, with all of the horrifying cases of child abduction and molestation we hear about. Our government has also taught us not to trust, especially after September 11. We cannot trust people who look a certain way or who are from a certain nationality or of a particular religion; they might be terrorists! At the supermarket, post office, or other public place, if you try to make eye contact with anyone, they tend to look back at you as though saying, "What do you want from me?" This builds the energy of lack of trust.

Many times I hear from people who want to go with me to one of the Intensives I hold around the world, but they don't because of lack of trust. They can't trust the airline, or the food, or the people, or they don't want to travel alone because of fear. Huge issues of trust are always lingering around. In business, especially in a corporate environment, you specifically learn not to trust. If you do, your competitor or even coworker will steal your ideas and benefit, so you had better keep them secret!

Sometimes during my classes, students may be in the flow and receiving wonderful information, but then they stop the flow by wondering if the information they are receiving is truly coming from the Lords of Akasha. They started questioning the source and wondering if they are making it all up. They tell me that the way they receive the information is similar to the way they have received before, and this makes them doubt that it is coming from Akasha. I tell them that it makes perfect sense that it would occur that way. We are using the senses to translate the information, and the senses are linked to the base of knowledge that we already have. If you have studied metaphysics for many years, the information will come to you in a language closely related to metaphysics. The same will be true if you are an architect or an engineer. The information will be filtered through your personal knowledge base and presented in a language that you can understand. I ask my students, "Is the information you are receiving beneficial and enlightening?" The answer is usually yes. If this is the case, continue with the flow, and trust. Remember that a lack of trust will get in the way of allowing.

You may be wondering how the process of receiving information from Akasha works. When we open our Akashic Records, we are tapping into a very high frequency, which we must adjust to. The frequency or energy slowly descends to our eighth chakra. The eighth chakra is the first of the transpersonal chakras. (I will explain the chakras in more depth in Chapter 19). The energy then slowly comes down to our open seventh chakra, touching upon the crown as a gentle waterfall that continues descending to our heart.

Once the energy hits the physical level, even at the subtle level of the seventh chakra, we start using our senses to decode the information. When the energy enters your eighth chakra, it is encoded Sacred Geometry, or Light Language. This is the way in which Spirit communicates with us. I am sure you have seen paintings from Renaissance artists such as Giotto di Bondone or Botticelli, or perhaps modern artists such as Alex Grey, in which a halo is depicted around a subject's head. The halo represents the light descending around the crown chakra. From this point down, the information is decoded. Sometimes you can even see words of fire that look like Hebrew, Sanskrit, or Hindi inside the halo.

We use our senses to help us create thoughts, mental images and words, so that we can describe and write down the information we are receiving. As no two people are alike, no two people will receive the information in exactly the same way. If you are auditory, you will be able to hear the information as words. If you are visual, you will be able to see the information as images. If you are tactile or able to sense energy, you will be able to feel the information being received. These are the senses that people have predominately developed to connect with Spirit. This doesn't mean, however, that the other two senses cannot be developed to give you a more complete way of receiving information from Akasha. Your sense of smell and even taste will increase as you work with the Records, bestowing a greater dimension on the information you are receiving.

Most people have one sense that is more developed than the others, but we all use them in the same way. We open them and fine-tune them to receive the information from Akasha. If you start getting your information visually and you want your other senses developed, ask the Masters and Teachers to start increasing the volume of all of your other senses while you are in the Records. If you do this, ask for it to be done gently and easily. Create a scale from one to 10, with one being very weak and 10 being maximum strength. If your hearing is at an eight and your other senses are down to a two or three, or maybe even a minus three, as you sit with the Records energy, you will gradually feel how the other senses start coming into play. When all of your senses are at an equal volume, your experience in the Akashic Records will have a different "flavor." You will experience a more extraordinary and complete way of receiving, expanding you to the next level of your connection with the Masters and Teachers, and giving you more each time you open your Akashic Records.

This is an invaluable tool when you learn how to open the Akashic Records of others because it will make the information that is being channeled for them more accessible and complete. This is Level Two material, though, so for right now the most important thing for you to learn is to open your own Akashic Records for personal healing and growth. For now it is all about you, because you must create the space that will allow you to interact with others. You must first have personal healing, explore the depths of your psyche, and create a strong relationship with Akasha.

The process I have described here can be called channeling. Believe it or not, channeling is something we do as children when we communicate with our unseen friends. It is natural, part of the standard equipment we are all born with. Little by little, however, we forget. We start creating separation, layers like filters that eventually stop the flow completely. The job of the channeler is very similar to that of a translator or an interpreter. They simply allow themselves to sense the communication from Spirit. The channeler attaches words to the information being received for understanding by themselves and others.

At this point, I am sure many of you would like to open your Akashic Records even though you haven't finished the book. That is understandable, as you have the Sacred Prayer, the formula, and the AAA recipe. If you are going to go ahead and open your Records, I suggest you proceed to Appendix B and answer question number one. This is the first question I ask my groups when I am teaching, and I think it is a wonderful question to explore. Here is how:

1. Write the question down on a piece of paper and answer it. Yes, just like that, without your Akashic Records open.

2. Write for approximately four to five minutes and then stop.

3. Bring yourself to center. Do a mini centering meditation and your AAA recipe on page 132.

Once you know you are ready, open your Akashic Records.

Read the question again and answer it. What you will find is an open flow of communication or information that moves effortlessly. You will be able to feel the shift of energy that comes from being in the Records. Write for approximately 15 minutes, then stop and close your Records. Depending on the way you receive information, you will be able to see, feel, or hear the Masters. Most people start writing as if someone were whispering words in their ears or projecting a movie in front of them, and the only thing they are doing is describing it on paper.

After this initial question, you are on your own. I let go of your hand and allow you to explore and create a personal relationship with the Masters and Teachers. I fully trust that this adventure will be amazingly rewarding in your life. However, if you need me, I am always around!

THE FOUR OTHER PRAYERS

FORGIVENESS PRAYER

If there is anyone or anything that has hurt me in the past, knowingly or unknowingly, I forgive and release it. If I have hurt anyone or anything in the past, knowingly or unknowingly, I forgive and release it, for the highest good of others and myself.

The healing power of this prayer is limitless. Your past consists of anything prior to the breath that you are taking right now. If you say this prayer at the end of the day, it clears the energy of the day of all the tidbits of negativity that build the walls of separation within and between us. Working with this prayer for 33 days consecutively has proven, in many cases, to heal insurmountable chasms of pain and separation in relationships with self, God, and other people and situations in our lives. We don't even have to know what is there; we just have to be willing to forgive. Forgiveness is the key that opens the floodgates of love and compassion.

PRAYER FOR RELEASING OUTSIDE INFLUENCES

If what I am experiencing is not mine, may God have His shield around me and I release whatever it may be to Him.

This prayer can be used at any time one feels a physical sensation (somatic/ emotional/mental) that may be empathetically taken from someone else. Empathic absorption is done in an effort to understand or relieve the burden or pain of someone else. This unconscious action is not a service to God, others, or you. Use this awareness to help that person and yourself release all to God. Therein lies the healing.

PRAYER FOR LOVED ONES AND ENTITIES

Father/Mother/God, we ask that this entity/soul be sent on its spiritual evolution for the highest good and mutual benefit of everyone concerned.

Sometimes when we open the Records, we may feel there were a block against or interference in connecting to the information available. This prayer releases that energy back to God so the information can flow unobstructed. An entity is an energy-form that is attracted to the light. It is not a form trying to enter or possess your body. An entity may be a part of an addiction that comes to take your light, however. A soul is the energy of a loved one who may be seeking completion with a person so that it may continue on its evolutionary path. This prayer may also be used on a personal level to release any energy that interferes with your own personal evolution or advancement.

PRAYER FOR PERSONAL CLEARING

I ask God for His shield of Love and Light to illuminate my path. I ask for clarity so I may be able to see with my inner and outer vision and clear all obstructions and obstacles from my life.

This is a powerful prayer that can be used to clear patterns of interference. You can use this prayer before you open your Akashic Records to bring you to center, to give you clarity, and to clear all that might be in the way of deeply connecting to the Records.

⌁

The four prayers presented here can be used inside or outside the Akashic Records. If you are in a situation that requires immediate attention and you don't have the time or don't want to open your Records, you can still use these prayers quite effectively.

19

The Chakras

Within every living person there exists a series of energy fields, very much like generators, that are called chakras. They exist on the subtle rather than the gross or physical level. Asian cultures have known about these centers for more than 2,000 years, but it's only in the last two decades or so that this information has come to the West. In Sanskrit, the word *chakra* means "wheel," and so they are conceptualized as spinning wheels. These energy centers are located within the body, in the front and the back of the spinal column. Each chakra has its own color and vibrates at a specific frequency. In our work with the Akashic Records, we are addressing these centers of energy. We can directly or indirectly energize and balance the chakras as we do our work, with the use of intention and the assistance of the Akashic energy. One of the functions of the Akashic Records energy is to bring your chakras into alignment as it descends down your body. You can visualize this energy as a liquid light coming through you to align all of your energy centers.

For our purposes it is helpful to understand the basics of the chakras, including their functions and the qualities that manifest when they are underactive or overactive. Once you learn the function of each chakra and its relationship to the human body, you will then be able to extrapolate that relationship to the one you have with life itself. Using the Akashic Records, you can create a line of questioning about your relationship to your chakras. For example, you may ask what your relationship is to the world through your first chakra and then explore the way you relate to physical survival, health, and other first-chakra issues. Later, I will provide some questions that will help you develop this art and deepen your experience.

The chakras work both independently from and in relationship to one another. For example, the first and seventh chakras work together, and having these centers in balance unites heaven and earth. The tube or channel that houses the chakras runs right up the middle of the body, from the first to the seventh chakra. This tube is called the *Sushumna,* and it is the central channel of energy. It is associated with Saraswati, the Goddess of knowledge, music, and the arts in Hinduism. She is the consort of Brahma, the creator. This channel is also known as the dural tube. This tube connects the sacrum with the cranium, and cerebrospinal fluid flows through it 24 hours a day, from birth to death.

The second and sixth chakras work together. Creative energy enters the second chakra and flows straight up to the sixth chakra, the third eye, for expression. The third and fifth chakras work together. The third chakra is the seat of the emotions. As they build up there is a need to express them, so the energy moves to the fifth chakra, the throat, to be released through verbal expression. The fourth chakra is the master, the director of all energy in the system. It is the only chakra that works by itself. It radiates energy up and down the body for a deeper connection with the earth or the Divine. The fourth chakra has two chambers: the upper chamber, which connects us with divine love; and the lower chamber, which connects us with human love.

THE MAJOR CHAKRA CENTERS

FIRST CHAKRA: BASE OR ROOT

The first chakra is red and it is located at the base of the spine. It is the chakra closest to the earth and the root or center of all physical experience. The basic issues and fears of this chakra revolve around security, food, and shelter; these are our fundamental concerns of physical survival. Our fears regarding physical survival, abandonment, and loss of physical faculties influence all of our daily thought processes. So the primary function of this chakra is for the security of our physical existence. This involves our family, the safety of friends and loved ones, and the ability to provide for life's necessities. It controls the fight or flight mechanism. It is the chakra of physical survival.

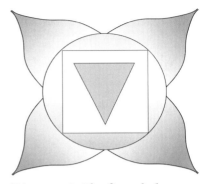

Diagram 8. The first chakra.

Psychologically, this is the center of the altered ego, where you are concerned with your own thoughts and feelings, sometimes to the exclusion of or indifference toward those of others. It's all about you. Your survival and your possessions come first, and it is best that no one gets in your way because you are creating a reality to conquer the world; you want to control and hoard. One of the main problems of the individual acting from first chakra motivation is violent behavior based on insecurities and fears about basic needs.

SECOND CHAKRA: SACRAL OR NAVEL

The second chakra is orange and it is located between the base of the spine and the navel. It represents our sexuality, sexual impulses, and creativity. This chakra's focus of attention is sexual energy, sensual desires, and fantasies. It is the center of procreation. When we operate primarily from this chakra, we see the world in terms of our desires, and our main motivation is to make sure that our desires—usually for relationships—are gratified.

The energy in this chakra is connected to the primal, reptilian brain at the base of the skull, emerging from the spinal column. The main responsibility of this part of our brain is to ensure dominance and survival of the species. Clearly the first and second chakras are intimately connected.

Diagram 9. The second chakra.

THIRD CHAKRA: SOLAR PLEXUS

The third chakra is yellow and it is located in the solar plexus area, behind the navel. This is the seat of emotions, feelings of personal power, anger, and

Diagram 10. The third chakra.

hostility. Our intuition is stored here, as well, and as such it is the center of psychic-etheric intuition. It is the seat of emotionally driven living. No wonder we use the phrase "gut feeling"!

Someone who has a dominant third-chakra personality is someone who utilizes fire and intellect to achieve his or her goals in an extremely competitive, assertive, and courageous way, sometimes without considering the consequences. When dominated unconsciously by the passions of this chakra, the individual begins to sacrifice family and friends in search of power, respect, and recognition. Unbalanced third-chakra energy results in a person who is willing to run over others to achieve his ends. Control of others is often maintained through fear, violence, anger, resentment, vengeance, and inflamed emotions. For individuals with an out-of-balance third chakra, there is never enough fame, fortune, power, or control over others and their physical environment.

FOURTH CHAKRA: HEART

The fourth chakra is divided into two chambers, the upper chamber and lower chamber. The heart chakra is located in the center of the chest, *not* where the physical heart is. The lower chamber connects us to human love, and its color is green. The upper chamber connects us to divine love, and its color is pink. In the middle of the two chambers is an altar, the secret chamber of the heart called *chante ishta* in Lakota, the center or eye of the heart and the place of union between the upper and lower chakras. On this altar rests the three-fold flame, a tiny flame with three plumes: Love, Wisdom, and Power. If we have a balanced threefold flame, we have a balanced life. The heart chakra as a whole is the center of love, harmony, and peace; indeed, and it is through this chakra that we fall in love.

Though ultimately we fall in love through the fourth chakra, this is not how we first feel attraction. When we see someone we are attracted or drawn to, that energy registers on the second chakra, the center of sexual attraction and passion. If and when feelings develop, the energy moves up to the third chakra, the center of feelings and emotions. As those feelings grow, the energy eventually moves to the lower chamber of the heart chakra, and we identify what we feel as love. Sooner or later, that energy moves up to the fifth chakra, the center of self- expression, and we express what we feel in our heart. If we are lucky, the other person is going to accept what we are expressing with an open heart and tell you that he or she feels the same way. As time goes by, the energy moves to the sixth chakra, the center of vision. We start creating the imagery of the future. If you have a partner who shares a spiritual life with you, you will be able to move the energy to the seventh chakra to connect at a deep, intimate,

Diagram 11. The fourth chakra.

and spiritual level. As all of this takes place, the energy of the crown chakra sends a signal to the first chakra to anchor the experience in the physical plane. All of the energy is returned to the heart for complete union between upper and lower chambers. Keep in mind that as a relationship progresses, the energies will continuously move through all the chakras, imprinting on them as you experience a deeper connection with your partner.

The upper chamber of the heart is reserved for your connection with divinity. Here is where you go to deeply pray, to meditate, to connect with your spirit friends and guides. And here is where we go to develop a relationship with the Lords of Akasha, and enjoy a meaningful spiritual experience.

Out of this union, and when we raise our conscious energy to the heart chakra, we set foot on a true spiritual path. This chakra is a matrix of nurturing, caring energy and the seat of the higher emotions of love, compassion, kindness, and empathy. Consciously operating daily from the heart, our energy, thoughts, and actions help us transcend the lower-chakra issues that can keep us stuck in Samsara forever. Here we can attain an integrated balance between the three lower chakras and the three upper chakras. When we learn to operate from the heart, and we create a heart-centered practice such as opening the Akashic Records, we are able to remove the material that holds us back. Attachments fall away, and true compassion surfaces in our lives.

The human heart beats approximately 72 times per minute, adding up to 100,000 beats every day. Five to 25 quarts of blood pulse over 60,000 miles of veins, arteries, and capillaries *every minute*. When we learn to meditate from the heart, when we are willing to look closely at the relationship we have with this chakra and to let go and heal all of the wounds associated with the heart, what we discover is that that heart chakra has a deeply profound influence on our overall health. It is in this chakra where blood and air (*prana*) unite, and this keeps body and mind energized and purified. As the heart pumps, it generates the strongest electromagnetic field produced by the body. This electromagnetic wave vibrates the 60 trillion cells in the body on an average of 60 to 70 times per minute. These frequencies are 100–1,000 times greater than the electromagnetic frequencies generated by our brains; they can even be measured radiating up to 4 feet away from the body! Imagine the impact you could have in the world if you consciously developed the wisdom of your heart.

At the end of this chapter I will share with you a beautiful meditation practice that will help you purify your heart and bring more love and compassion to your life.

FIFTH CHAKRA: THROAT

The fifth chakra is located within the throat and its color is blue. It is the center of communication, self-expression, and judgment. If you experience any problems with your throat, you can draw the color blue to this area and it will help you say what needs to be said. The fifth chakra needs a lot of attention and

healing, as it has been abused and misused for centuries. The patriarchal societies that have developed over the past few centuries have suppressed the divine feminine. Men have overused and abused this chakra, whereas women have underused it, sometimes out of fear of losing their lives. Unfortunately, this pattern is still prevalent in many cultures today.

The fifth chakra relates to communication and growth through expression. The emotions for the fifth chakra are faith and understanding. This chakra is parallel to the thyroid, a gland that produces

Diagram 12. The fifth chakra.

a hormone responsible for growth and maturation. Physically, this chakra governs communication; emotionally, it governs independence; mentally, it governs fluent thought; and spiritually, it governs a sense of security. It plays an important role in the art of lucid dreaming, chanting, toning, singing, and speaking with conviction and truth. The vibrations of all these activities affect the body down to the cellular level. This is also the first of the chakras we've looked at that focuses *primarily* on the spiritual plane.

SIXTH CHAKRA: THIRD EYE OR BROW

The sixth chakra is located at the center of the forehead and its color is indigo. This chakra is used to examine and question the spiritual nature of life. Our inner vision is also contained here, including inner gifts of clairvoyance, wisdom, and perception. Visions and dreams are held in this chakra, as well. This chakra is symbolized by a lotus with two petals. It is at this point that the two sides, *Nadis Ida* and *Pingala*, are said to terminate and merge with the central channel, *Sushumna*, signifying the end of duality.

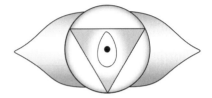

Diagram 13. The sixth chakra.

Every time we breathe, both air and ether travel along either the Ida nerve or the Pingala nerve; after circulating up and down, it then passes through the nostrils. The Ida nerve begins in the left nostril, at the root of the nose just where the left nostril converges into the right, passes through the cerebellum and medulla oblongata, runs along the left side of the spinal cord, and ends at the lower end of the spine. Similarly, the Pingala nerve begins in the right nostril, passes through the cerebellum and medulla oblongata, runs through the right side of the spine, and ends at the base. Within the root of the nose, where the two nostrils converge and where Ida and Pingala begin, is one of the vital spots in the body.

As I mentioned previously, the Sushumna is a canal. Though not directly connected with either of the nostrils, it begins at the base of the brain, that is, the medulla oblongata, and runs down the central cavity of the spinal column and ends at the coccyx, where Pingala, Ida, and Sushumna connect. The Sushumna is also known as the dural tube that houses the spinal cord.

The seed syllable for this chakra is the syllable *om*, and it is here where we can balance our male and female energies. This chakra is about balancing the higher and lower selves and trusting inner guidance. It is through the third-eye chakra that we are able to create what we see within ourselves. This chakra is responsible for our ability to look within, create a vision, and then manifest that vision outwardly in our life. This third-eye chakra is also linked to the pineal gland. The pineal gland is a light-sensitive gland that produces the hormone melatonin, which regulates sleep and waking. The third eye has to do with accessing our intuition. Mentally, it deals with visual consciousness; and emotionally, the it deals with clarity on an intuitive level.

SEVENTH CHAKRA: CROWN

The seventh chakra is located at the top of the head and its color is violet or white. It is the chakra of divine purpose, the chakra of destiny. It is the doorway to Spirit and the transpersonal chakras. It balances the interior and the exterior, bringing them into a harmonious whole. In Sanskrit this chakra is called *Sahasrara*, which means "1,000-petal lotus." It is considered the chakra of pure consciousness. This chakra has no sound; it is complete silence. When male and female energy rise in purity from the base of the spine, a state of liberation occurs as the energy hits the seventh chakra; for many, this is the Kundalini rising and symbolizes the Shiva and Shakti energy uniting as one. This chakra is about inner wisdom and the death of the body, the place whence we can attain liberation at the moment of death. Sahasrara's inner aspect deals with the release of karma, physical action with meditation, mental action with universal consciousness and unity, and emotional action with a pure state of being.

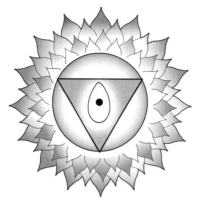

Diagram 14. The seventh chakra.

In Tibetan Buddhism, the point at the crown of the head is represented by a white circle. It is of primary importance in the performance of the Phowa practice, consciousness projection after death, in order to obtain rebirth in a pure land. When this chakra is open from practicing Phowa, a small bump, a drop of blood, or even an opening may appear on top of the crown, where a small blade of grass is then inserted.

THE EIGHTH CHAKRA AND ABOVE

The eighth chakra and above are the transpersonal chakras, our true connection with the Divine and the Masters and Teachers. From these chakras, we experience grace, ecstasy, and spiritual union with God.

CHAKRA QUALITIES

FIRST CHAKRA (RED)

The first chakra, located at the level of the tailbone, brings vitality or life-force into the body. It controls the consciousness of survival and well-being.

Overactive:	Underactive:
Paranoia	Apathy
Aggression	Weakness
Mania	Depression
Nervousness	Passiveness
Fear	Self-destructiveness

To balance: Close your eyes and place your attention directly on this energy center. In your mind's eye, see this bright, fiery red center about 4 inches in diameter, spinning evenly and smoothly like a perfectly balanced sphere at the base of your spine. Envision this sphere drawing in conscious energy to stimulate physical well-being, health, self-love, and vitality. Imagine a feeling of profound security rushing through every cell in your body, leaving you feeling calm, confident, and protected.

SECOND CHAKRA (ORANGE)

The second chakra, located at the level of the sexual organs, focuses on the physical plane and the senses of the flesh. It is the seat of sensuality, emotion, pleasure, and creativity. When someone's second chakra is balanced, he or she enjoys life, feels happy, takes great pleasure in sensual experiences, and is creative.

Overactive:	Underactive:
Greediness	Disinterest
Addiction	Repressed feelings
Anxiety	Self-deprivation
Compulsiveness	Depression
Frustration	Denial of bodily pleasure

To balance: Close your eyes and place your attention on your midsection between your navel and your tailbone. In your mind's eye, see this fiery orange energy center spinning around and around, perfectly balanced. As it rotates, see it warming your whole body and filling you with self-appreciation and pleasure. Let the energy flow through you and into every cell in your body, warming and burning all the dark, tense, cold places.

THIRD CHAKRA (YELLOW)

The third chakra is located at the level of the solar plexus. It is the seat of the emotions and connects feeling with personal will. It is the seat of focus, decision, volition, and willpower. When this chakra is balanced, the person feels confident, decisive, focused, and committed to his or her path.

Overactive:	Underactive:
Subjectivity	Wishy-washiness
Bossiness	Inability to concentrate
Narrow-mindedness	Naiveté
Abrasiveness	Passiveness
Dictatorship	Obliviousness, ignorance

To balance: Close your eyes and place your attention on your navel, the center of your body. In your mind's eye, see a bright yellow sun radiating brightly. Imagine it is rotating in a perfectly balanced way. Imagine that as it spins, the energy of direction, confidence, support, and focus are being drawn into you. Let this vitality fill every cell in your body, moving you toward your highest possible good, free from any and all emotional baggage.

FOURTH CHAKRA (GREEN)

The fourth chakra is located at the level of your heart in the middle of your chest. It connects you to vibrations of love, security, contentment, and benevolence. It is the seat of the soul, the location of the sacred altar of the heart, and the center of love in your consciousness. Love is always patient, calm, generous, and kind. It is accepting of oneself and others.

Open Heart Chakra:	Closed Heart Chakra:
Balance	Sadness
Patience	Loneliness
Kindness	Suspicion
Generosity	Neediness
Peace	Possessiveness
Humor	Bossiness
Forgiveness	Greediness

To balance: An open heart chakra radiates love and creates connections with people, animals, and the planet as a whole. The heart chakra radiates the warmth of love, and this warmth can actually be felt through the hands. To balance the heart chakra, bring your full attention to your heart and visualize a vibrant color green. Imagine a sphere approximately 3 inches in diameter, and allow it to gently spin, growing and becoming warmer. As the chakra gains momentum, feel it drawing in soothing, healing energy, melting away all fears and wounds and replacing them with loving, caring vibrations. Feel the energy of the Masters and Teachers and the unconditional love they give you. Take it in so you can then share it with the world.

FIFTH CHAKRA (BLUE)

The fifth chakra is located at the level of the throat and controls the psychic consciousness of hearing. This includes telepathy as well as hearing the guiding wisdom of your soul. This ability is called *clairaudience*.

Overactive:	Underactive:
Distraction	Dishonesty
Negativity	Willfulness
Resentfulness	Hostility
Preoccupation with others	
Gullibility	Confusion
Abusive language	Repressed Emotion

To balance: Bring your attention to the center of your throat, and visualize a vibrant blue sphere, spinning in perfect balance. As this sphere rotates, imagine it pulling in the energy to allow you to speak clearly, resonating with only the highest, most honest and loving ideas and words. See divine energy soothing your throat, guiding both inner and spoken words for your highest good.

SIXTH CHAKRA (INDIGO)

The sixth chakra vibrates the color of a deep indigo blue sky. It is located at the level of your eyebrows in the center of your forehead. Also known as the third eye, this chakra governs imagination, ideas, visualization, and the psychic awareness called clairvoyance. This endows one with the ability to see auras, chakras, and spirit guides.

Overactive:	Underactive:
Hallucination	Lack of imagination
Paranoia	Insensitivity
Day dreaminess	Self-absorption
Tendency to space out	Narrow-mindedness

To balance: Center your imagination on the area of your forehead between your eyes and visualize a beautiful indigo sphere of about seven inches in diameter spinning smoothly. As it spins, imagine it filling your mind with beautiful healing images. Imagine playing in a field of poppies like a free-spirited child. Now imagine that your soul is looking upon you with loving energy and deep affection. Do not force this image. Instead, gently allow it to emerge from and then fade into an indigo mental screen.

SEVENTH CHAKRA (VIOLET/WHITE)

The seventh chakra, also called the crown chakra, is located at the highest point of our body at the crown of our head. This chakra is connected to the pineal gland and governs the consciousness of spiritual awakening, inner wisdom, and enlightenment. Opening the seventh chakra can bring sacred energies to the heart. Regular meditation, prayer, and opening of the Akashic Records can help to open and activate this center. This opening can be maintained if the desire is true and the intention stays focused on love, compassion, and service.

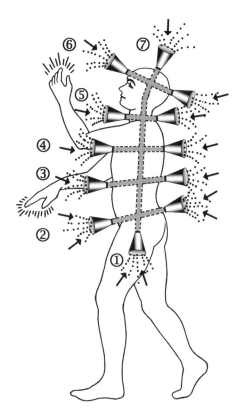

Diagram 15. The chakras and their energy flow.

HEART CHAKRA MEDITATION

The following meditation comes from HH Sogyal Rinpoche, and it is based on the Tibetan Buddhist practice of Tonglen. Tonglen is the practice of taking the suffering and pain of others and giving them our happiness, well-being, and peace of mind. Tonglen utilizes the breath. As Geshe Chekhawa wrote: "Giving and receiving, should be practiced alternately, this alternation should be placed on the medium of the breath" (from *The Tibetan Book of Living and Dying* by Sogyal Rinpoche, p. 206).

Some of you may be thinking how hard it must be to take the pain and suffering of others, without first strengthening your own kindness, love, confidence, and compassion. It is your relationship and trust in the Masters of the Akashic Records that will give you the confidence in this practice and the power to transmute pain and suffering into happiness and well-being. Make sure you practice first with people you know, with friends and family, before you move to other people or people who are truly sick, suffering, or in pain.

In Tonglen we take on, through a compassionate heart, all the various conditions that make people suffer. We can take all the mental and physical suffering, fears, frustration, pain, anger, guilt, bitterness, doubt, and rage and give them, through love and an open heart, all of our happiness, well-being, peace of mind, healing, love, and fulfillment.

A POWERFUL SECRET

You may be asking yourself, *If I take in the pain and suffering of others, won't I risk harming myself?* If you feel that you don't have the capacity at this moment to do this, if you don't have the strength, courage, and compassion to do this practice, don't worry. Just imagine yourself doing it, saying in your mind, *As I breathe in, I am taking on the suffering of my friend; as I breathe out, I am giving him/her happiness, love, and peace.* Just doing this simple breathing exercise will inspire you and build your confidence for the more in-depth practice.

Remember, any feeling that you generate has to be first owned by you. So, by generating a strong feeling of love, kindness, and compassion, you are equipping yourself to relieve the suffering of others. In the words of Sogyal Rinpoche:

> *The one thing you should know for certain is that the only thing that Tonglen could harm is the one thing that has been harming you the most: your own ego, your self-grasping, self-cherishing mind, which is the root of all suffering. For if you practice Tonglen as often as possible, this self-grasping mind will get weaker and weaker, and your true nature, compassion, will be given a chance to emerge more and more strongly. The stronger and greater your compassion, the stronger and greater your fearlessness and confidence* (Ibid., p. 212).

If we have been created in the image of God, we have it in our power to do as He does.

Loving as He loves,
Helping as He helps,
Giving as He gives,
Serving as He serves,
Rescuing as He rescues,
Being with Him 24 hours,
Meditating as He meditates,
Praying as He prays,
Touching Him as He touches hearts and minds.

Open your Akashic Records and bring your complete awareness to your heart; there, start generating the feelings of love and compassion, and see them as a ball or sphere of pure white light. Through this practice, your focus shifts from interest centered on the personal self and its selfish interests, to understanding that the greatest source of satisfaction in life comes from helping others experience well-being and happiness.

Begin this practice by visualizing someone whom you love unconditionally, perhaps a child, whom you truly wish to relieve of any type of suffering. Visualize breathing in her pain or suffering as a dark, smoky cloud leaving her body. Breathe the dark smoke into the white light of the heart chakra, where it is instantly transformed into sparkling bright *prana*, or life-force. Exhale that sparkling white cloud of prana, sending it toward the other person. See the beloved enveloped in healing, bright white mist. Continue breathing in the dark smoke and exhaling out white light until you feel that she is are completely purified and established in peace and happiness.

Next, focus on someone else whom you love, but might have issues with, and repeat the previous sequence with him. After that, you can focus on individuals who have hurt or betrayed you, followed by individuals you do not like and may even hate.

Finish the meditation by focusing on your heart and the feelings of love, kindness, and compassion. Feel as if all were bathed in the white light of your heart chakra.

20

Grace and Grace Points

Grace is the freely given favor and love of God/Spirit/Source that is used to regenerate and strengthen humans. All of us have the ability to open up and ask for this grace to come in. The only thing you have to do is ask, and then be willing to receive and be in gratitude.

Grace is mentioned in all sacred scriptures, whether Christian, Protestant, Islamic, Judaic, or Hindu. In the Hindu faith, *bhakti* is translated as "devotion" and involves the practical involvement of the individual in divine communication with the gods. Within *bhakti*, we find what is known as *kripa*, or divine grace. This is the ultimate key required for spiritual self-realization. Divine grace is developed from a pure heart devoted to a spiritual path, generating sufficient energy for us to have that kripa. Kripa is the key to our spiritual enlightenment, realization, growth, and connection with the Masters and Teachers of Akasha. You may think of grace as the light, a powerful cosmic, spiritual energy that has the power to change our lives.

Let us look at the difference between light and grace.

Light is:

- The radiance, illumination, or luminosity from a particular source.
- The state of being visible, exposed to view or revealed to public notice or knowledge.
- Mental insight, understanding, and clarity.
- Spiritual illumination or awareness; enlightenment.

Grace is:

- The freely given gift or favor and love of the Creator Spirit.
- The influence or spirit of a power greater than yourself operating in people to regenerate or strengthen them.
- Divine love and protection bestowed freely on people.

MY EXPERIENCE OF GRACE

I thought I had an understanding of grace because I had read about the lives of many mystics from the East and West and their descriptions of grace. I have had many remarkable spiritual experiences in my life, that I can call transcendental, but one truly helped me understand the meaning of grace. Around the time I was exploring the forgiveness issues I mentioned previously, I was engaging in very deep meditation and inner exploration, and I had an experience that took me into a place completely different from anything I had experienced before. When I came out of this experience and regained my center, I felt that my whole body was luminous with a golden radiance I had never felt before. I felt clarity, peace, and a love so great it was almost hard to contain. For years I have tried to put the totality of this experience into words and have not been able to do so. The only thing that I know is that my life changed as the result of it. I call this experience grace.

Right after this experience, the one thing I really wanted was chocolate! I had never liked chocolate very much. I was in my early 40s at the time, and during my entire life up until that point, I could have had a little piece of chocolate and been satisfied for six months. After this experience, however, I wanted chocolate immediately. The bottom line was I just had to have it, so I drove to the closest gas station and stood in front of the candy bar section like a wide-eyed child in awe of how many varieties they had. I had no idea what any of them tasted like, so I ended up buying one of each. In the next 24 hours I consumed them all! The discovery of this delicious gift from the gods began my new love affair with chocolate. Now it is almost mandatory that I come to my Akashic Records classes prepared with chocolate to pass out to all of the students. I have come to the full realization that whenever we do deep spiritual work, we must eat some chocolate. By the way, chocolate is a wonderful way to ground yourself if you feel a bit spaced out after spending time in your Akashic Records—all in moderation and balance, of course!

GRACE POINTS

Grace Points have been given to us from the Akashic Records as physical points of action. They stimulate movement of energy on different levels of the human being (physical, emotional, mental, spiritual, conscious, unconscious, and genetic) so that we may return to a place of peace and alignment with the divine will. Both processes—stimulating the movement energy and returning us to a place of peace—support us in reaching our highest potential in all endeavors. Access to the Akashic Records and the Grace Points were given in order to assist us in three ways:

1. **Gaining clarity:** Use your intention and moderate pressure on the Grace Points to redirect the conscious mind to access the information you are seeking. Asking for clarity allows movement within consciousness to open you to a new awareness or truth.

2. **Releasing that which no longer serves you:** Use your intention and moderate pressure on the Grace Points to release limiting conditions, patterns, false beliefs, past judgments, etc., and allow movement and transformation of stationary energy. Releasing limitations allows a shift in consciousness to replace a *contracted memory* with an uplifting memory. (A contracted memory is a memory that was created via a contract in the present or a past life. Many times the contract has already expired, but the energy of it still lingers in the mind. A good example of this is someone who gets divorced because of infidelity. The original marriage contact was created out of love, but the divorce came about because of the infidelity. The imprint of infidelity will block that individual in future relationships, unless the imprint created in his or her mind is dissolved. When we consciously dissolve an existing contract we have the opportunity to create a newer one that serves us better in the present.) Releasing these old patterns helps to expand your comfort zone by bringing more balance to your inner state of being.

3. **Integrating that which serves you:** Use your intention and moderate pressure on the Grace Points to integrate new information and

insights, imprinting positive experiences and awareness into your being. This includes all information that brings you into a place of love
and divine awareness.

I view Grace Points as an escape valve for energy, similar to the valve of a
pressure cooker. Just as we put all the ingredients for the recipe into the pressure cooker, we put all of the ingredients of our emotional life into our subconscious. If we don't do something to neutralize and let go of the energy after an
emotional episode, it goes into our own personal pressure cooker. As we move
through life, we turn up the heat. Over time the water comes to a boil and the
stuff inside begins to cook. The building pressure needs to escape somehow
(this is what the little valve on top of the lid is for), but if we don't have a way to
let the emotions go, we will explode. That explosion can come in the form of a
meltdown, a full-fledged nervous breakdown, or worse.

Grace Points act as a pressure valves when we are receiving information
from the Akashic Records. Grace Points are not active all the time. They become active as the result of energy being taken in or subtle emotions and memories surfacing due to the questions we are exploring. Grace Points have a masculine or feminine component, depending on the type of issue we are working
with. Grace Points that manifest on the left hand have feminine components
and qualities. Grace Points on the right hand have masculine components and
qualities. To know if a Grace Point is active while you are exploring a question
in the Records, all you do is you touch it. Press Grace Point #1 hard with your
thumb. For Grace Points #2 and #3, pinch with about 20 pounds of pressure.
This is equivalent to the amount of pressure you apply when opening the lid of
a new jar. If the Grace Point is tender, this means it's active.

Let's say you are exploring an issue that has to do with your mother. You
find that Grace Point #2 is very tender on your right hand, but not your left.
Here's why this may be the case. As I mentioned, Grace Points have masculine
and feminine components. You would expect Grace Points on your left hand
to be very tender because this issue seems to have to do with a direct feminine
influence. However, when you check the ones on your right hand, lo and behold, they are really tender. How can this be? The right hand represents the
masculine, but you are working on mother issues. It is possible that during
the time the cellular imprint was created, the mother energy was very weak in
comparison to the energy of the father. Perhaps your father made your mother
administer the discipline, even though it hurt your mother immensely to do it.
Perhaps your father was so domineering that she felt she had no choice. In this
case, you received the direct impact from your mother, but the original source
of the energy was your father. This could explain why the Grace Points on your

right hand are tender rather than those on the left. Things were more complex than they originally appeared. In this way, the Grace Points provide a beautiful thread to follow to get to a point of complete clarity and healing.

Now that we have an idea of how to use Grace Points #1 and #2, let me explain Grace Point #3. Imagine you are a woman going to a family wedding. The whole family is going to be there, and you are already predicting what your parents and other family members are going to say about the life path you have chosen. You go to the event with your girlfriend, so you know your family will have something to say about it. They know exactly where, when, and how to push your buttons. Even if you don't bring a date, you know they have enough material from the misconceptions they have about you to trigger you. Even before you get to the event, there is a buildup of emotions inside of you, but you have no other choice but to attend. As you arrive and your family starts throwing energy at you, Grace Point #3 comes to the rescue. As you will find out soon, Grace Point #3 helps to release issues, judgments, beliefs, and emotions that have been passed down through your genetics or ancestry. As you work with the Grace Points on both hands, you are disconnecting from the dynamics and energy that are taking place during the conversation in a very direct way. You are actually healing as you disconnect.

If you want to begin doing ancestry or genealogy work, you had better be ready, because it is very powerful and will bring up many emotions. It is a wonderful opportunity for you and any other family members you want to join you. You don't even have to tell them what it's all about. The energy itself is sufficient. If a situation similar to what I described previously occurs, it can give you powerful material to explore with your Akashic Records. Later on, I will give you a couple of juicy questions about genealogy.

While you are exploring an issue like this with your Akashic Records, the Masters may guide you to have a conversation with your mother and or father to tell them you are divorcing them. You are creating a separation from their toxic energy, and you need to move away from their beliefs and into your own. I actually did this when I was 16 years old, and it has given me immeasurable freedom in my life. For some people this process may be very difficult but also very necessary. Remember that the familial and cultural programming you've experienced may not be helping you or supporting your spiritual evolution.

Divorcing your parents doesn't mean you will never see them again. It only means you will create the necessary energetic distance to explore your freedom. I know from experience, and I have witnessed this with my students, that your parents will see you change. They will see you as happier, more fulfilled, more successful, more peaceful, more loving, and more compassionate. All of this will impact them at an energetic level. More than once I have seen this actually lead the parents to reunite with their son or daughter and ask questions and seek guidance about their own lives. In this case, you can actually tutor them and balance the karma between you in a positive way. Again, this is powerful and beautiful work full of opportunities for all concerned. In the Akashic Records Level 3 class we deeply explore this material (see Appendix D for more information).

The last thing that I would like to mention here is that as you do ancestry work, not only do you heal the present, but you heal the past and create new possibilities for the future. Be aware that if past-life memories surface with negative episodes related to family, be very careful because the perpetrator could have been you. Now you are back to look at whatever happened at that time and bring it to full resolution.

THE AKASHIC RECORDS LEVEL 1 GRACE POINTS

THE MAIN GRACE POINT

- Clarifies the information being received
- Releases any issues, judgments, beliefs, emotions, etc., concerning the soul's evolution (past, present, and future), thereby clearing any resistance
- Integrates the new insights, creating positive reference points

BODY RELEASE GRACE POINT

- Releases any physical pain or discomfort
- Releases energy that is being held and clarifies the source of pain or discomfort
- Gets energy moving from the body part as we ask for clarity from the Records

THE GENETIC (ANCESTRY) LINEAGE POINT

- Clarifies the information being received
- Releases issues, judgments, beliefs, emotions, etc. that have been passed down or taken on
- Integrates new aspects of being

How do you know when the energy has been completely released from a Grace Point? When you check it again and the tenderness or pain is gone, or when you feel a big sigh or body tremor, then you know the energy has been released.

HOW TO WORK THE GRACE POINTS

Hold a specific Grace Point and focus your intention on it. Focus your intention on that which you want to release and surrender. Relax and feel grace flow throughout your being and melt the emotion tied to the issue.

Use Grace Points with specific words or prayers, like the ones included in this book, to assist in focusing your attention and intention. For example:

> *I release and completely let go of my (physical, mental or emotional body/soul, genetics, or ancestry) past, present, and future, any and all fears, false beliefs, and judgments and any and all limiting patterns regarding _____. I surrender and let go of this now and let it go to grace, to Source, to be replaced by divine love and light.*

Now sit in the energy, let it go, and relax.

Use your intention and the touch of the Grace Point to redirect your conscious mind to access the information you are seeking. Ask the Masters and Teachers for clarity while touching or pinching the Grace Point, and allow for the cellular repatterning within you with new awareness and insight.

- ☙ **Grace Point #1:** The Main Grace Point is located in the center of the palm.
- ☙ **Grace Point #2:** The Body Release Grace Point is located on the side of the palm between the small finger and the wrist.
- ☙ **Grace Point #3:** The Ancestry Lineage Grace Point is located in the webbing between the thumb and the index finger.

All Grace Points can be used inside the Akashic Records. Using the Grace Points when you have your Records open and are in communication with the Masters and Teachers is the actually most effective way of using them. However, you can use the Grace Points outside the Akashic Records in just about any situation.

Let me give you an example, using Grace Point #1. Imagine you are on your way to an important lecture, and the speaker will be presenting material that you know will enrich your life, business, spirituality, whatever. However, you went to sleep late the night before and you had to drive three hours to get to

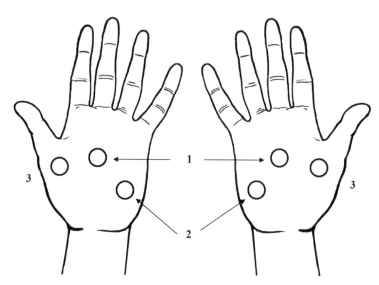

Diagram 16. Level 1 Grace Points.

the venue. When you arrive, you are tired and can hardly keep your attention on the topic being presented. In this situation, you can use Grace Point #1 on both of your hands as you listen and receive the information. Remember that Grace Point #1 is for anchoring and clarifying information being received. In a way, it is like a personal tape recorder. Information will flow directly to your subconscious mind, bypassing the tiredness that you feel. Later, through the Akashic Records, you can ask for that information to surface so you can use it in a practical way.

Let's look at another example, this one using Grace Point #2. Let's say you decide to go to Bali. To make this journey, you have to take three or four planes, and you have several layovers and long flights on top of all of that, but it's worth it. You are on one of the legs of your journey and your lower back starts hurting. The pilot has made the announcement that you have to have your seat belt on and remain in your seat, so you can't get up and walk around a little bit to stretch. In this situation, you can use Grace Point #2 to clear the energy. Start working on this point on both of your hands as you bring your attention to the body part that is aching. Little by little, like the steam escaping from the pressure cooker, the buildup of energy in your lower back is going to start to dissipate.

Grace Points are a wonderful gift from the Masters of Akasha that support us in our process, both inside and outside the Akashic Records. We have learned the three basic Grace Points from Level 1, and by now we are clear about how the Akashic Records allows us to gain self-awareness through our questioning. This awareness assists us in understanding how we co-create our lives. Our growth, awareness, and wisdom come through physical experiences. What we do with those experiences and how they direct our growth is up to us. Our work in the Records will bring us into alignment with God/Spirit/Source. We do this through grace. Grace is the gift of Spirit. The more we open up, and the more we allow ourselves to surrender to higher wisdom, the more we will experience the right outcome and healing in our lives.

Using the Akashic Records, we uncover the motivations of the ego, which affect how we experience and relate to love. The ego affects the way we love and nurture others and ourselves, as well as how we experience abundance, health, harmony, and happiness. The ego is not a negative aspect; it is merely a support mechanism that brings all of the shortcomings we need to overcome into our conscious awareness. Without it we would be blind to these opportunities. By using grace, we move into redirecting the mind/ego/emotions to support peace. When we move into grace, we actually experience an internal state of peace. This allows more freedom in conscious choice. This inner peace becomes our reference point for our connection to God/Spirit/Source, which we can use to resolve issues or conflicts and bring greater alignment into our lives. We can accomplish this by holding the intention of grace while physically activating the Grace Points in our hands.

Using the Grace Points is simple, really. Medium pressure to the Grace Point, your intention, and allowing are all that are needed. Doing this redirects your consciousness so that you can release what is no longer needed to God/Spirit/Source and integrate all that you desire. The intentional choice of grace allows the flow of energy for clearing and alignment and directs the clearing all the way down to the cellular level. As you will see, establishing an inner reference point to peace is an ongoing process of discovery.

And now, because I am being guided to do so, I would like to share with you the Grace Points for Level 2. This will give you even more information about the use of Grace Points.

Grace Point #1, Emotional Release Point: Directs the consciousness to disconnect and clear emotions. It is located in the pad below the small finger.

Grace Point #2, Cellular Level Clearing Point: Directs the consciousness to disconnect and clear on a cellular level. It is located in the pad area between the two middle fingers.

Grace Point #3, Ego Disconnect Point: Directs the consciousness to disconnect and clears the ego. It is located in the pad below the index finger.

Grace Point #4, Reconnecting Original Innocence Point: Directs the consciousness to move to our original innocence. It is located in the lower palm in the pad area above the wrist.

Let's explore these four Level 2 Grace Points in greater depth.

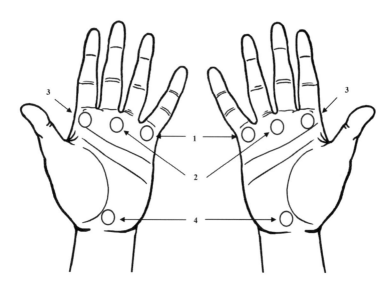

Diagram 17. Level 2 Grace Points.

EMOTIONAL RELEASE POINT

If you are exploring an issue in the Akashic Records and an emotion is brought up that needs to be cleared, the Emotional Release Point is the Grace Point to use. This Grace Point will help you disconnect the emotion from the issue you are exploring. As mentioned previously, the Grace Point can be active in either hand, depending on the original energy.

Let's look at an example. Imagine you are working on the issue of a broken relationship. You are still in the relationship, but it is obviously coming to an end. As you move in the direction of finalizing this break, many emotions arise, such as great sadness, anger, dissatisfaction, failure, self-image issues, and un-worthiness. Opening your Akashic Records can provide a profound source of understanding. The Masters will guide you in the direction you need to go to bring about a loving completion. While you are in the Records working on this, you can use Grace Point #1 to disconnect any emotion tied to the issue. It is like pulling a lamp plug out of the wall. The lamp stops receiving the electricity to function and the charge dissolves.

Any emotion that comes up that is not supporting your life can be released through this Grace Point. Remember that Grace Points can be used inside or outside the Akashic Records. In another example, if you are attending a business meeting and someone says something that gets your blood boiling, before you start engaging in negativity and getting into an argument, use Grace Point #1 to clear the emotional charge out of your field.

CELLULAR LEVEL CLEARING POINT

The Cellular Level Clearing Point is a wonderful Grace Point to use when you are exploring issues deeply connected to your cellular memory that you need to release. Here is an example of how issues can be connected to cellular memory. Let's say you are in a new relationship and things are going great. You open your Akashic Records to ask for guidance so you can continue nurturing the relationship in a positive way. While in the Records, memories and the energy from previous failed relationships come up. You take the time to explore the possible causes of these failures and discover that a breakup when you were a teenager has been impacting you all this time. The emotional imprint from the experience was taken so deep, it went into your cellular memory. With this awareness, you can start using these Grace Points to clear the imprint from your cellular memory.

The Masters may also remind you of any arguments you witnessed between your mom and dad in your childhood, arguments that led to relational breakdown or even divorce. This type of scenario commonly creates an imprint at a cellular level and can be the cause of difficulties in personal romantic relationships. It may also cause difficulty in making commitments. Again, the Grace Points can be used to release these emotions from your cellular memory.

Here is another example. Imagine you are 6 years old. You are in kindergarten and you really enjoy it, but your teacher is a bit angry and impatient with the children. One day she passes out watercolors, places a vase of flowers and fruit on her desk, and asks the class to paint it. You feel like Michelangelo. You see yourself with a painter's hat, a palette in one hand, and a paint brush in the other—you are creating a masterpiece! You are in the flow of energy creating with joy and freedom when the teacher walks by and stops to look at what you are doing. She says, "That doesn't look at all like what is on my desk," and then she simply walks away. That 10-second interaction with your important teacher figure creates an imprint that both shames and crushes you. You put the brush down and feel as though all the air had been sucked out of your body. Your inspiration and creativity come to a screeching halt. This episode creates a cellular imprint that will prevent you from expressing your artistic abilities with complete freedom in the future.

You may have guessed that this is actually a personal example. I actually had this experience when I was 6 years old. When information like this surfaces from the Akashic Records, you have the perfect opportunity to release the cellular memory connected to the issue using your Grace Points. When this memory came up for me and I cleared it, I felt as though I had received a shot of creativity. I bought acrylic paints and started painting everything I could find.

I started using remnants of leather to paint and this evolved into my leather-work craft, making handbags with beautiful beadwork patches for the flaps. The practical application of healing, once the cellular memory was cleared, transformed into my leatherwork business, which made me great money and brought happiness to the many people who purchased the items. I know they can feel the joy and love that I put into my creations.

EGO DISCONNECT POINT

The Ego Disconnect Point is a juicy Grace Point to work with because it is directly related to the altered ego. We have all engaged in the use of the altered ego at one point or another. Are you the type of person who always has to be right? Maybe you are having a conversation with a group of friends and you not only defend the point you are making but also fight to make sure you are proven right, no matter what. In a situation like this, it would be useful to use the Ego Disconnect Point. This point will help make you more humble and receptive.

As I mentioned before, you will get a lot more out of the material presented here and in many situations if you enter with a beginner's mind. If you enter the work from the expert mind, you are also entering with a certain amount of ego. In this case, you may find yourself thinking things like, I've done that before. I already know that. The expert mind is centered on the altered ego, and there is little room for anything new to enter it because it is already full. You may have seen this orientation in some actors, doctors, lawyers, politicians, spiritual gurus, and CEOs who see other people as beneath them and don't treat them with kindness and generosity. Anyone who gets trapped by the altered ego at any point can benefit from working with this Grace Point. Some people may have to work harder than others to get this energy clear and under control.

Here is another way this Grace Point can come into play. Imagine you attend a class and you have a breakthrough that gives you a glimpse of enlightenment. You can own your experience and talk about it, but it is very important to pay attention to how you are talking about it. Are you letting your ego tell the story, or are you allowing the humble part of yourself share without attachment and engagement of the ego? If you find yourself in the altered ego, inside or outside of the Records, you have a wonderful opportunity to use this Grace Point.

RECONNECTING ORIGINAL INNOCENCE POINT

The Reconnecting Original Innocence Point is a great Grace Point to use when you are exploring the inner child. In the example I gave you earlier about the child in kindergarten whose artistic expression was crushed, in addition to using Grace Point #2 to clear the cellular memory of the experience, you would also use this one to reconnect and integrate childlike qualities that were once lost. In other words, you can both clear the cellular imprint and reintegrate new energy so that you can put what you are receiving immediately into use.

Think of the anecdote I related earlier in the book about the child going to the supermarket with his mom and almost getting hit by a truck. If this type of memory comes up, you can use Grace Points as part of your soul retrieval. You can use the Reconnecting Original Innocence Point to reconnect the memory to the present moment and integrate the childhood energy. Your inner child may require some kind of physical action or expression. Be prepared to welcome the inner child. Be prepared to celebrate and do some childish things. Be prepared to look foolish in the eyes of others as you bring more joy, passion, play, and spontaneity into your life.

21

Journaling

Last, but certainly not least, an incredibly important aspect of this work is journaling. Learning to journal your experience with the Akashic Records and using this skill for your own spiritual edification will be a major part of your experience. Journaling creates a personal link to your own spiritual source. It provides a way to communicate with that source and creates a database of your experiences. This is the best way to have information available to you for the future, because the Masters will give you a lot of information! Many times it will be a precise recipe, and you will want to remember all of the details of what you receive so you can take action.

A diary is a book, notebook, or planner in which one records events, usually written in a plain, brief, and superficial manner. A journal is a book, notebook, or any collection of written thoughts where one writes about events in more detail. This especially includes feelings, opinions, hopes, fears, beliefs, reflections, and so on. A journal is a powerful tool to help you tap into your imagination and evoke personal change. The Akashic Records offer a way of journaling that will help you to take a close look at yourself and assume your role as the main character in your life. Journaling and writing will help you attain joy by shaping your life's experiences, moving you through what causes pain into an outcome of self-knowledge and a point of perspective.

Journaling is like the script a director needs to direct a play. By now we know that we have to separate ourselves from the drama of life to become both the observer and the director. Without a journal, without the script, the director cannot direct or make any changes to the drama as it is unfolding before her eyes. So, just as the script is essential for the play, journaling is essential when you are receiving information from the Akashic Records. Every time you open your Akashic Records and communicate with the Masters and Teachers, you should keep a daily log or a list of thoughts and quotes to remember.

Once you establish a flow of good communication and relationship with the Masters, they will give you so much information that will be invaluable in many areas of your life. I know from personal experience that it is extremely difficult to remember it all, especially as time passes. It is a lot like going to the movies. When you see a movie you really enjoy, a certain imprint is created from the visual, emotional, and visceral impact of the movie. When you go to work the next day and tell your friends about it, you can provide a wealth of details and share your excitement. About a week or two later, if someone asks you about the the movie, some of the details will already have been lost. About a month later, if you want to tell someone about it, you might not even remember the name of the movie. If so many details are lost after a month, imagine how little you'll remember six months or a year later. If you see the movie again, you will most likely say, "Oh my god, I had forgotten all about that!" If it is this way with a movie, imagine how it will be with the information that flows from the Akasha, information that is like a recipe you need to follow step by step. Keeping track of it can only be accomplished through journaling.

A practical benefit of journaling is that you can gain access to your subconscious mind and create a future by conscious choice. By reviewing the information you journal, you can make better decisions. Keeping a journal can change your life, and journal therapy is a tried and true way to help you solve your problems.

To help students get comfortable with journaling during my classes, I give them an assignment that I'll share with you. Place a letter-sized note pad on your nightstand next to your bed. In the morning, right as you wake up before you get out of bed and get distracted, take the note pad and write two full pages of information, whatever comes to mind. If you are like me and are not a morning person, this will be difficult. Regardless, take the pad and start writing anything at all, even if it is something like: "This just doesn't make any sense to me. I am way too sleepy. I would like to go downstairs and get a cup of coffee. This is a dumb exercise and I don't want to continue doing it. This is a waste of my time." At some point your conscious mind will give up and the superconscious will take over. It will continue writing without your really knowing what you are writing. Finish your two pages and go on with your day. When you come back home, pick up the pad and start reading. You will immediately discard all the nonsense and come across the gems, jewels that surfaced from your superconscious mind. This is a good exercise to do with your Akashic Records open because it will help you with the flow of the pen on the paper. It will help get your conscious, critical mind out of the way and allow the information to flow from the Akashic Records as you continue receiving information from the Masters.

Top 10 Reasons for Journaling

1. **Find yourself:** Discover who you really are by recording your feelings, thoughts, opinions, beliefs, hopes, fears, experiences, etc. Writing in-depth to yourself about yourself helps clarify who you are, what you believe, and what you want to do with your life.

2. **Become organized:** When you know yourself clearly by writing honestly and in detail, your mind becomes focused. You feel more at peace with yourself. Journal writing can organize your daily mundane life, as well. By recording things that you need or want to do, you know where you're going. Journal writing helps you stop, think, and plan carefully.

3. **Solve problems:** Getting all of your thoughts on paper can make you think in new ways by tapping into your subconscious. This allows you to see a problem in a new light and find solutions for it.

4. **Increase creativity:** Jot down inspiring thoughts or ideas and collect them. Certain writing techniques can help you tap into your subconscious and inspire you, including the Akashic Records, poems, short stories, drawings, music, or whatever you like to do to express yourself. The act of writing allows you to think and concentrate such that that your mind works at a deeper, more intuitive level.

5. **Find sanctuary:** Writing to yourself in your journal is a great way to escape from chaotic feelings or events, or just escape from the mundane feelings of everyday life, and delve into a more exciting inner life. Separating yourself from the outside world gives you a stronger sense of your own identity as an individual human being. Taking time for yourself also generates a great sense of peace and well-being, thereby boosting your confidence and self-esteem.

6. **Get emotional therapy:** Your journal can act as your own best friend or a proverbial shoulder to cry on. It is always there to listen and never criticizes or talks back. By unburdening yourself with difficult thoughts or feelings, you lower stress. Problems don't seem so bad when they become mere words on a page.

7. **Enjoy life:** By recording things that make you happy, listing your favorite things about being alive, and celebrating the good things in your life, you become a happier person. You become more appreciative and grateful for what you do have, rather than depressed for what you don't. Writing your perceptions of life also gives you a better sense of the world around you and your place in it. Even the most mundane things can become profound and meaningful if you take the time to use all of your senses and record what you experience in your journal. Writing about the little things in life makes you feel that you are living life to the fullest and experiencing everything life has to offer. Each of us has our own unique sense of perception and set of experiences, so use your journal to celebrate your uniqueness.

8. **Record your time line:** As you keep a journal over months and years, it becomes a record of your accomplishments, travels, and personal growth, much like a time capsule that has captured who you were at certain moments in the past. Recording the who, what, when, where, why, and how of past events helps you to remember details you probably would have forgotten had you not written them down. Having a record of what you did with your life gives you a feeling of accomplishment and a feeling that your life was not wasted.

    Journaling can also help you create a bucket list, a list of all the things you want to do and accomplish before you die. These things can range from places you want to visit in the world to knowledge that you want to acquire.

9. **Communicate better:** Without even realizing it, writing in your journal regularly will improve your writing and communication skills. You will become better and better at expressing yourself. Writing in a journal is much like talking to a close friend or telling a story. Having your thoughts organized on paper allows you to communicate those thoughts in a clearer way, whether speaking or writing.

10. **Create a personal/family history:** Keeping a journal during the course of your life creates a valuable record of who you were, what you did, what you thought, what you liked and disliked, your superstitions and quirks, and so on. It's a record of your identity. A journal is a link to the past. Someday the present we are living in now will become the distant past. Writing a journal is also a link to the future.

Epilogue

The distinction between the worldly and the spiritual is neb-
ulous, as the spiritual and the material are deeply interrelated.
The life we live either reflects this essential harmony or is full of
seeming contradictions and challenges that call for introspection, understanding, and self-realization. The Akashic Records
reconnect us with the present moment of experience and allow
us to recognize the deep and meaningful connection we have
with the Divine. The Records also open our eyes to the past and
give us the means to heal any and all issues. They provide the
tools for us to move into the future with freedom.

As people embark on a spiritual journey, they may grapple
with the dimensions of the worldly and spiritual and feel the
separation between the two. It is my hope that this material will
allow them to see that there is no division at all, that we operate
on this physical plane because it is here, in the physical, where
we need to embody our spirituality and integrate it into daily
life. It is in this plane of existence that we can let go of the past
and fully embrace the future, and where we can let our light
shine in the present. As we let our light shine, we are examples
for others to do the same.

The Akashic Records and all of its attributes impress upon us the idea of an honest and complete human life. The Akashic Records are at the center of an evolving humanity and they bring a practical interpretation and inspiration, as well as instruction for living a well-balanced and practical life. Embodied within this wisdom is a spiritual impetus that compels us to live a life of truth and constantly seek higher wisdom. Let the Akashic Records be your companion and your guide. Create a deep and meaningful relationship with the Masters and Teachers, and trust that they are here to support you in your life.

⚬

In closing, I would like to share a beautiful poem that could be your motto in life. This poem is directly related to the first question I ask when I teach the Akashic Records workshops. Do you remember it? The question is, "What makes you beautiful, talented, gorgeous and magnificent?"

> *Our deepest fear is not that we are inadequate.*
> *Our deepest fear is that we are powerful beyond measure.*
> *It is our light, not our darkness that most frightens us.*
> *We ask ourselves, Who am I to be brilliant, gorgeous, talented, fabulous?*
> *Actually, who are you not to be?*
> *You are a child of God.*
> *Your playing small does not serve the world.*
> *There is nothing enlightened about shrinking so that other people won't feel insecure around you.*
> *We are all meant to shine, as children do.*
> *We were born to make manifest the glory of God that is within us.*
> *It's not just in some of us; it's in everyone.*
> *And as we let our own light shine, we unconsciously give other people permission to do the same.*
> *As we are liberated from our own fear, our presence automatically liberates others.*

—From *A Return to Love* by Marianne Williamson

Think of every word of this beautiful poem and see where you hold back. See if you shrink to accommodate others in your life, if you have the fear of not being accepted by others, and how much you buy into the energy of victimhood instead of the energy of your powerful presence and magnificence.

Think about these words: *Our deepest fear is not that we are inadequate. Our deepest fear is that we are powerful beyond measure.*

Because you have sought this book out, I am going to assume that you are searching to reawaken your personal power. If this is the case, I can assume that this fear about your personal power has come up.

It is our light, not our darkness that most frightens us.

The moment that you start embracing your power, as you develop a deep connection with spirit, with Akasha, you will start shining your inner light. As this light shines, you start changing, and other people will notice. This most likely will scare you because you are not used to the feeling of this inner light.

We ask ourselves, *Who am I to be brilliant, gorgeous, talented, fabulous?*

Wounds from the past come up; the inner saboteur will start a conversation with your ego; and they both will win if they can keep you small.

Actually, who are you not to be?

That's right! Who are you not to be?

You are a child of God.

Do you fully believe this? If your answer is yes and it comes from the heart, then what is the excuse you have not to assume the role of child of God in this life? If you own the feeling of truly being a child of the Divine, then you must act like one, behave like one and accept all the richness that this world has for you.

Your playing small does not serve the world.

If you want to make a positive impact in the lives of others, if you want to live your life to make a difference, then...

There is nothing enlightened about shrinking so that other people won't feel insecure around you.

Embrace your inner light, have the courage to change, to heal, to transform yourself and be an example to other people of the magic of transformation through the Akashic Records. Don't hide your spirituality; don't create a split in your life by not living your life like a child of the Divine. Become whole and fully integrated and share it at the office, in your home, with friends, with strangers.

We are all meant to shine as children do.

Imagine that you can return to childlike innocence. Imagine that you are carefree and light, free from the delusions of the world. Imagine God/Goddess provides for you always, and you move to a space of complete trust. From that space you are not afraid to shine. Your light becomes so bright that you scorch the shadows of your interior and exterior world. You are free.

We were born to manifest the glory of God that is within us.

That's right: We were born to manifest the full glory of God in every aspect of our lives—our inner life, our financial life, our relationships, our health, our friendships, our devotion, our career, our fun, our play, and our overall enjoyment of a well-balanced life.

It's not just in some of us; it's in everyone.

We all have the same initial imprint, or seed, of the Divine; it is in all of us. The Buddha said that all living beings have the potential to attain Buddhahood. Jesus Christ said, "I say unto you, He that believeth on me, the works that I do shall he do also; and greater works than these shall he do."

And as we let our own light shine, we unconsciously give other people permission to do the same.

We must do this. We must let our light shine and in so doing illuminate our lives and the lives of others. This light will be our guiding light at all times in the dark days and empty nights that are a part of the process of life. We have this inner light to guide us.

As we are liberated from our own fear, our presence automatically liberates others.

Liberation is actually the bottom line, our own personal freedom and the development of wisdom, compassion, love, and gratitude. By owning this energy, by embodying it and operating from the heart, we will constantly emanate the energy that will nurture the seeds of possibility in others.

- ✦ Have the courage to look within.
- ✦ Don't remain in doubt and fear.
- ✦ Gain confidence in self-liberation.
- ✦ Embody your beauty and magnificence.
- ✦ Be happy and share it with the world.
- ✦ Don't be afraid to love because, at the end, that is all that matters.

Appendix A
How Did We Receive the Akashic Records Prayer? The Story of Johnny Prochaska

The story of Johnny Prochaska began long ago in Spain. Johnny was the son of a Spanish nobleman of Czechoslovakian lineage, an aristocratic family that placed extreme importance on their properties and other material possessions. They had this privileged position for many generations, so their lifestyle was ingrained in family history. Johnny had a sister named Mary and a younger brother, Peter. Johnny was the oldest of the three children, and he was expected to learn and play the role his father was showing him, in addition to special lessons that he was receiving at school.

Their home was an modernized family castle with beautiful gardens, horses, and spacious rooms. The inside of the house was decorated impeccably with a modern Spanish style and a blend of other European influences. The family had a staff that kept everything running smoothly including gardeners, maids, men that took care of the stables, and of course a nanny for the children. One nanny in particular had been with the family more than 50 years and had seen two generations grow up. Her name was Rachel.

Rachel knew that the Prochaska family was going to have a special child, and so she knew she had to wait until the child was born to recognize him. Rachel was an unusual woman. She was very well organized and clean, but she also had unusual abilities that allowed her to move rapidly from one place to another, almost as if she were gliding above ground. Because of her unique way of being, she moved from being a maid to being in charge of all the servants. What she enjoyed the most, however, was taking care of the children. She kept waiting for a sign of this special little one's arrival.

Importantly, Rachel was a member of an ancient hermetic esoteric society. She had learned the wisdom of the ancient ones and, through her connection with spirit, she knew her role in that house. The Prochaskas were kind and grateful for Rachel's presence in their home. She always seemed to know about things before they happened, and would warn of oncoming difficulties. Her hunches always seemed to be right. When she first started working at the house this ability astonished people, but little by little, they all got used to it and enjoyed living with the wisdom of this woman.

When Johnny was born Rachel just knew that this child was a special one. Knowing that there would be more children, however, she waited to see him grow up. Mary and Peter came along and, although they were beautiful and radiant, they did not have the inner sparkle that Johnny had. From an early age Johnny loved to spend time with Rachel in the kitchen, telling her about his visions and connection with the animal kingdom. He was able to communicate easily with birds, squirrels, lizards, rabbits, and all of the other animals, and they all seemed drawn to Johnny. For him there was nothing unusual about this; when he was around animals, he always had a most unusual glow. Rachel always said that Johnny exuded a green and vibrant field, a glowing emanation that always surrounded him.

It was not unusual to see Johnny playing by himself in the gardens and having conversations with his unseen friends. While Mary and Peter always played together in the house with all the beautiful toys that money could buy, Johnny spent most of his time either outdoors communicating with nature or in the kitchen sharing his discoveries and adventures with Rachel. Rachel not only listened to Johnny, but also taught him a lot. She opened him up to the wisdom of spirit and tutored him in esoteric teachings that were appropriate for his age.

Johnny's mom and dad tried and tried to bring him inside the house, buying him toys and games, but they just could not get him in the house. They could also sense something unusual, almost magical, about this child, and many times they came to Rachel for advice because they knew that Johnny and Rachel were very close. Rachel's advice to the Prochaskas was to let him be. She said that he was a special child, one who, when the time was right, would bring a very special message to the world. He would share the wisdom of the stars for those who were ready to receive it. The Prochaskas did not understand this at all, but they knew there was something different about Johnny because as much as they tried to make him similar to Mary and Peter, nothing worked.

After the Spanish Civil War, when the country was recovering, the political and financial situation in Spain became very difficult for the Prochaska family. Mr. Prochaska experienced severe financial setbacks, and he could see even more difficulties in the future. So he consulted his financial advisers. He was in the kitchen sitting deep in thought when Rachel came to him and said, "I know that your heart is heavy and carrying a big burden. You are receiving mixed signals. Your heart tells you one thing and your advisers, another. Know that their advice comes from personal interest. If you make the decision you know you have to make, their lives will change and their advice is based on the fear of personal loss and personal interest." She also said, "Change is the only constant thing in life. Change is what gives us experience. Change, when it is well-grounded, is what makes the man. Listen to yourself and honor what you hear." Mr. Prochaska was speechless. No one, including his wife, knew of the meetings or the approaching difficulties that he could see for his factories and farmland, but Rachel knew. How did this old woman know? How could she give such specific advice that went deep into the core of his being?

Mr. Prochaska said to Rachel, "Old woman, you have seen me grow up and now you are seeing my children grow up. I don't know where you get your wisdom and how you always know what the best thing is for my family. If I do what is in my heart, it will disturb the lifestyle of the family; and besides, I don't even know where to go."

Rachel replied, "You are right—most of them don't know about this, but there is one that feels the change, and that one is Johnny. He knows. This move will change the destiny of your family. This change will redirect the mission of the stars. The cosmic counsel of the four and 20 elders and the Lords of Akasha are all behind what you're feeling in your heart, and a place has been secured for you in the new world."

"The new world!" Mr. Prochaska exclaimed, "What do you mean by that?"

Rachel answered, "This is the place of ancient civilizations, the place of cultures that we have never understood, and the land of opportunity and growth for you and your family. This is the place of magic, where people are communicating with nature, spirit, and land. It is a place of color, spontaneity, purity of heart and devotion, and a place of simplicity. This is where your oldest son will receive his message, the message from the stars."

"Okay, Rachel," he said, "Where is this magical land?"

"Mexico," she replied.

After that they both went into a deep silence and Rachel left the room, leaving Mr. Prochaska alone to think. As she left the kitchen, she turned off the lights and lit a single oil lamp. The mood of the room changed. The walls started fairly vibrating with a golden light. The single light created a sense of expansion and, to Mr. Prochaska, it almost felt as if the kitchen's walls moved 20 feet back. Out of the golden glow a three-dimensional image appeared like a brilliant, colorful moving picture, unlike anything Mr. Prochaska had seen before. There he saw the land of Mayas, pyramids, and colorful people. As he looked around the kitchen, he was seemingly surrounded by these images. It was almost as if he were an outsider looking in.

He was able to see their homes, their lifestyles, the loving interactions among families and neighbors, and a colorful, abundant marketplace where people were peaceful and happy. He saw men busy working, building a pyramid, architects with simple measuring instruments, and a map of the stars. He saw people walking into a temple to pray, honor, and give thanks for what they had. He saw some of the elders, and to his shock and surprise, he saw his son Johnny as a grown man. Johnny was one of the seven priests initiating a ceremony in one of the pyramids, the one in between the sun and the moon. The vision shocked him and made him vibrate all the way down to the core of his being. Right then he understood Rachel's words, and he made the decision to move his family to Mexico City.

Mr. Prochaska went to his wife the next day and told her, "We are moving to Mexico City." When this announcement was made to the whole family, Johnny became more and more excited. He felt as if he were being called home. Right around that same time, Johnny started having a reoccurring dream. The dream was of him, late in the day, walking down a dimly lit cobblestone street and passing a door where an old Indian woman was standing. He could not make sense of this dream, but he had it repeatedly.

Once the family arrived in Mexico City, they moved into an exclusive neighborhood with other aristocratic Spanish families. They started cultivating relationships and discovering the lifestyle in their new home and country. With this type of family, to maintain the cultural traditions of the family and the bloodline, individuals are required to get married within their own social class. Johnny, however, fell in love with a Mexican woman and married her. This was a disgrace for his family, so he was basically disowned.

Johnny moved to Texas and opened a business to import goods from Mexico to the United States. On one of his business trips, one of his meetings was canceled and he found himself wandering the streets of downtown Mexico City. It was late in the day; the street was dimly lit, narrow, and paved with cobblestones; and as he continued walking, he passed a door where an old Indian woman was standing. He took two or three steps beyond the door and he suddenly stopped and realized that he was *living his dream*. He turned around and went back. The old Indian woman was sitting inside and asked him to come in. Johnny immediately saw the resemblance between this woman and Rachel.

The old Indian woman asked Johnny to sit down and told him she had been waiting many years for him. Johnny shared that he had had a recurring dream of walking down the street and passing the door where she was standing. The old Indian woman told Johnny that he had been selected to be the carrier of a sacred prayer that could change his life and the lives of others, but that this would require a great deal of responsibility. She asked if he was willing to be the carrier of the prayer and share it with others. When Johnny said yes, she asked him to follow her.

They walked all night to the pyramids of Teotihuacan. By the time they arrived, Johnny was tired and thirsty, so the old Indian woman found a place where they could rest. She gave him a piece of some kind of root that satisfied his thirst and appetite, and Johnny fell asleep. When he woke up, the old woman was already alert and waiting for him. She said, "Okay, it's time to go." They started walking in the direction of the pyramids, and as they got closer, Johnny started noticing there were other people walking in the same direction. These people were wearing different outfits from different cultures, and they were of different races.

Finally, they arrived at the foot of the Pyramid of the Sun, and they started ascending its steps. Once they got to the top of the pyramid, Johnny saw a group of priests and priestesses, and the old woman went to stand right next to the high priest. There she shape-shifted to become a young and beautiful counterpart to the high priest. The pair represented the male/female duality, the alpha and omega, the yin and the yang, the sun and the moon. The high priest told Johnny that he, Johnny, had been chosen to receive a sacred prayer that would forever change his life and the lives of others, so he had to choose very carefully. This was not a light decision to make. Johnny was told that he had to share and teach this prayer because the time was right for the world to start receiving this ancient wisdom.

The high priest asked, "Are you sure you're ready for this?"

Johnny replied, "Yes."

Johnny was placed in the center of the priests and priestesses, and a ceremony was begun. Out of Johnny's crown chakra a flame approximately 10 to 12 inches high appeared. The high priest took this flame with his hands, touched it to Johnny's heart, and then collapsed it between his palms. What appeared was a piece of gold paper where the Akashic Records prayer was written. The priest took this piece of gold paper and pushed it into Johnny's crown chakra, and the prayer melted into his being.

After this amazing experience, Johnny went back to Texas; needless to say, his life changed completely. It became an adventure of self-discovery. Johnny started teaching the Akashic Records prayer. One of the people to whom Johnny taught this prayer was a woman named Mary. Mary became Johnny's devoted student and friend. At some point, Johnny told Mary that his time was coming to a close and he had to pass the torch of the Akashic Records to someone else who could continue teaching this beautiful prayer to others. After he passed the torch of responsibility to her, one day Johnny simply vanished. Everything in his apartment was left intact. Many believe he moved back to Mexico; others believe that he simply ascended to a higher realm. Mary continued teaching the Akashic Records, and that is how I, Ernesto, came to learn about the Records. Here is how it happened.

In 1991 a friend of mine named Denise told me she was going to take a class on the Akashic Records and asked if I wanted to come along. I remember the first time I heard the word Akasha and how the vibration of the word gave me goose bumps all over my body. Unfortunately, I could not attend that weekend because I was teaching; however, Denise did attend. A few weeks after she took the class, she asked me if she could read my Akashic Records, and I said yes. I remember the kind, loving, and beautiful energy that emanated from the consultation, and how that energy enveloped me and made me feel loved. It was the kind of energy that was calling me home in a kind and loving way.

About a year later, Denise herself started teaching the Akashic Records. I took my very first class from her, moved up to levels 2 and 3, and then started assisting her in her classes. Right around the same time my then girlfriend started to teach the Akashic Records, and I started assisting her, as well. I just loved being in the energy! Both women constantly asked me why I didn't teach this material, and I kept saying, "No, I am too busy. I'm teaching other things. I don't have the time." Finally, one day while in my own Akashic Records, the Masters said, "How many times do we have to send you the message for you to get it? We want *you* to teach the Akashic Records!" As you can see, I am a little hardheaded sometimes.

I ended up calling Mary and expressed my desire to teach the Akashic Records. She told me she knew who I was; in fact, she had heard a lot about me. She said that I needed to schedule an appointment over the phone so that I could open her Akashic Records and read for her. She would then open her own Records and ask the Masters if I was ready. I told her in so many words, *Thank you, but that isn't good enough.* I wanted to fly to Texas and meet her in person. She agreed, and a couple weeks later, I went down to meet her.

I remember arriving in the morning, tired because I did not go to sleep early the night before. Mary picked me up at the airport and said to me, "You and I are going to start a new relationship. It is as if we were writing on a brand new page, completely free of what anyone has said about you or the way you read or assist during classes." We went to her home and I asked her if I could rest for a while before I opened her Records. She simply smiled at me, showed me the room where I was going to stay, and then showed me her office. She told me, "Put your things down and then come and see me." When I went to her office she was sitting and she said to me, "Okay, my dear, I am ready for you to open my Akashic Records." I told myself, *Okay, forget about getting some rest and go right into the reading. You can rest later.*

As I was preparing to open Mary's Records, the doorbell rang, and she said, "Excuse me, but that must be my friend who is coming to document the session." Not only was I nervous because I was going to read for Mary, but now I had an audience! At the end of the consultation, Mary said to me, "If you can teach half as well as you can read, you will be a wonderful teacher."

If lineage is important to you, as it is in many spiritual traditions, the closer you can get to the original teacher or Master, the less "diluted" the teaching is going to be. I am proud to say that I developed a close relationship with Mary, and she became my mentor and my teacher. In the lineage of the Akashic Records, I am a third-generation teacher, and that is very close to the original source: Johnny Prochaska, then Mary Parker, then my friend Denise, then me.

I would like to share with you the wise words that Mary had for me:

I truly appreciate your gentle, loving manner. You are using that to bring the knowledge of the Akashic Records and its practical applications out into the world. The way you teach your classes and lead your meditations is a modern approach to an ancient system of teaching. You have my blessings for all that you are doing with the Akashic Records. May you always and in all ways walk in God's Love and Light.

—Mary Parker

Appendix B
Questions for Connecting, Exploring, and Expanding

The following are some helpful questions and sub-questions to explore while using the Akashic Records. Explore the first question without having your Akashic Records open. Write for approximately five minutes. Then, open your Akashic Records and answer the question again.

QUESTION #1

- What erroneous belief operates in my life that causes me to experience the world in the way I do?
- Where did it originate?
- How do I release it, shift it, or heal it?
- Is there anything else I need to know?

An erroneous belief is a misconception resulting from incorrect information. It's something that you picked up from your childhood, family dynamics, peers, culture, social class, or general upbringing that is actively influencing your life at a conscious or subconscious level.

Some erroneous beliefs:

- Money is the root of all evil.
- I have to have a college degree to succeed in life.
- I must always please others no matter how I feel.
- I must be perfect in all things and at all times.
- I must always be strong.
- I must try hard at everything I do.
- I must be perfect to do spiritual work/healing.
- Women cannot attain as much as men.
- I am too young/old to start a new venture.
- The earth is flat.
- It is hard to make money
- I must have a lot of money to be happy.
- Others' opinions of me matter.
- We are all born with original sin.
- I am stupid/not good enough.
- I don't have the talent to play a musical instrument.

QUESTION #2

- What have been my primary challenges in my life, my main issues?
- What is the emotion tied to each situation?
- What is my ego connection to each situation?
- Where do I hold it in my body?
- How does it affect my work relationships?
- How do I best heal or change it?
- Is the core of this issue from this lifetime or a past life?
- Is there anything else I need to know?

QUESTION #3

- What is my inner child most afraid of?
- Where did it originate?

- ➻ Who was involved?
- ➻ How does it affect me?
- ➻ How does it hold me back?
- ➻ Where do I hide it in my body?
- ➻ How do I bring freedom to this inner child?
- ➻ How do I change it or heal it?
- ➻ What do I have to give my inner child in support of this process?
- ➻ Is there anything else I need to know?

QUESTION #4

- ➻ What is the pattern that I exercise most often in my personal relationships?
- ➻ What is the addiction?
- ➻ Where did this pattern originate and who contributed to it?
- ➻ What do I need to learn from it?
- ➻ How does it affect me in my life?
- ➻ Is this pattern meant to be altered or cleared in any way?
- ➻ If so, how? Can it be lifted or transmuted?
- ➻ Is there anything else I need to know?

QUESTION #5

- ➻ What is the greatest pattern of self-sabotage in my life?
- ➻ Where did it originate?
- ➻ How does it manifest?
- ➻ How does it play out in my relationships?
- ➻ What do I have to learn from it?
- ➻ How does it impact my life?
- ➻ How do I change it, shift it or heal it?
- ➻ Is there anything else I need to know?

QUESTION #6

- ➻ What do I have to do in order to create adventure and wildness in my life?

- What parts are missing?
- How and when did they become disconnected?
- How do I reclaim them?
- How do I give this process a physical expression?
- Is there anything else I need to know?

QUESTION #7

- What do I have to do in order to live to make a significant difference?
- What obstacles are in my way?
- Where do they come from?
- Are they attached to an individual?
- How do I clear them?
- Is there anything else I need to know?

QUESTION #8

- What is the greatest fear that keeps me from achieving my true potential in my life?
- Is it tied to a past life?
- Do I need to know about it?
- Is it tied to an event from my childhood?
- How do I remove the energetic charge from it?
- What do I do in the present moment to move forward without it?
- Is there anything else I need to know?

QUESTION #9

- What am I ultimately looking for in this lifetime?
- What obstacles do I encounter in my search?
- How can I best overcome these obstacles?
- What is the lesson for me?
- How do I best share this gift/talent with others?
- Is there anything else I need to know?

QUESTION #10

- In my most troubled relationship, what aspects of [name of person] are mirroring aspects of me?
- What do I have to do to heal that with him/her?
- Is this energy coming from a past life? If yes, ask questions to explore.
- [Bring the person into your mind's eye.] What does he/she need from me to heal?
- Is there anything else I need to know?

QUESTION #11

- What aspects of my soul have been robbed by others and how does this still play a role in my individual freedom?
- How do I put a stop to this?
- How do I reclaim the lost pieces?
- How do I integrate these into my life?
- How do I trust and best listen to my soul?
- Is there anything else I need to know?

QUESTION #12

- What subconscious patterns operate in my life in direct relationship to my first and second chakras?
- What do I fear the most about my personal survival?
- What am I afraid of losing?
- What do I lack to fully manifest my creativity?
- How do I best heal these aspects?
- How do I best share this with others?
- What do I have to do to fully enjoy life?
- Is there anything else I need to know?

QUESTION #13

- What patterns of procrastination do I carry within me that hold me back?

- Where do they originate?
- How do they hold me back?
- How do they affect me in my life?
- How do they affect my finances?
- How do they reflect in my personal relationships?
- Is this something that affects my personal growth and connection with Spirit?
- What do I have to learn from them?
- How do I best erase them from my cellular memory?
- Where do I hold them in my body?
- How do they affect my health?
- What do I do about this?
- How do I heal this?
- Is there anything else I need to know?

QUESTION #14

- What has been my primary challenge in this life coming from my ancestral history? (This is a question about genealogy or ancestry. Use your Grace Points as you answer it, referring to the diagrams on pages 160 and 162.)
- What is the emotion tied to this issue? [Use Grace Point #1]
- Where do I hold the energy in my body? [Use Grace Point #2.]
- How does it affect my mental, emotional, and physical health? [Use the appropriate Grace Point based on what answer you receive.]
- How can I best clear it at this time? [Use Grace Point #3.]

QUESTION #15

- What aspects in my genealogy or family ancestry are holding me back and what can I do to clear them? [Use your Grace Points here as well.]
- Is this connected to my father side of my family?
- Is this connected to my mother side of the family?
- How does it affect my emotional well-being?

- How does it affect my health?
- How does it affect my personal relationships?
- Is this affecting my children in any way?
- Is this creating codependency in my life?
- Is this energy keeping me from moving forward with my finances?
- What parts of my genealogy serve me?
- How do I best integrate this in my life?
- Is it for my highest good to disconnect from my ancestry?
- How do I begin to disconnect from it?
- Will this give me the personal freedom that I am looking for?
- Is there anything else I need to know?

Question #16

You are going to answer the next question with music. Before you read the question, put the book down and find a piece of music that is uplifting, that makes you feel wonderful and yummy—preferably instrumental music that doesn't have any singing or words. Once you have it ready to play, open your Records and answer while listening to the music.

- Show me my magnificence. How can I express this magnificence in my everyday life in a way I am not already doing?

Question #17

- What is the strongest animal alive? What qualities of that animal can I use in my life right now?

This is a fun question that I always like to ask in my Akashic Records Level 1 classes. I have answered this question dozens of times, and I always get a different animal; somehow it always relate to the energy that I need the most during that period of my life. Use your imagination, and don't be limited to animals that are alive; mythological animals many times come to lend their energy in the process.

Question #18

- What past lifetime can I connect to for strength, confidence, and self-empowerment?

- What do I need to know about it?
- How do I increase the energy that is within me from that lifetime?
- What did I learn then that I could utilize now?
- Would it serve me to know more about it? If yes, explore the details.
- How do I best integrate this energy in the now?
- Is there anything more I need to know?

QUESTION #19

- How do I tend to get caught up in the drama of life?
- Does anger, jealousy, sadness, depression, lack, abundance, or an altered ego trigger me?
- How does it trigger me in the way I respond to life?
- How does it affect me mentally and emotionally?
- How does it hold me back from peace, love, and enlightenment?
- Is there anything else I need to know?

QUESTION #20

- Bring to your mind's eye an image or picture of your mother. What feeling or emotion is present when you see her in relationship to your childhood?
- Describe the emotion.
- Where do I keep it in my body?
- How is this affecting my life right now?
- How is it connected to a past life experience with her?
- What happened then that can help me understand the emotion that I feel now?
- How do I let it go?
- Is there anything else I need to know?

QUESTION #21

- ↬ Bring to your mind's eye an image or picture of your father. What feeling or emotion is present when you see him in relationship to your childhood? Describe the emotion.
- ↬ Where do I keep it in my body?
- ↬ How does it play a balance in my life to maintain a masculine/feminine relationship within me?
- ↬ How is it connected to a past life experience with him?
- ↬ How is this affecting my life right now?
- ↬ Does it serve me?
- ↬ How do I let it go?
- ↬ Is there anything else I need to know?

QUESTION #22

Explore these three issues:

- ↬ Fear of abandonment
- ↬ Fear of trust
- ↬ Fear of not being good enough

QUESTION #23

Explore these eight worldly concerns that consume, create anxiety, and cause issues:

- ↬ Gain and loss
- ↬ Praise and blame
- ↬ Good reputation and bad reputation
- ↬ Pleasure and pain

Follow-up questions that will help you get deeper into the process:

- ↬ Can I move deeper into this energy?
- ↬ Can I move deeper into this question?
- ↬ Is there an underlying theme?
- ↬ Does this trace back to certain people or events?
- ↬ Can this be revealed to me at this time?
- ↬ Is there anything more?

↪ Is this past life related?

↪ Can you take me deeper?

↪ How do I heal it, change it, or release it?

If no words come up, write down feelings, emotions, and images. Be open to scents, visions, and so on.

10 more important questions:

↪ What is my life purpose?

↪ What is my passion?

↪ When I meet life's challenges, what is the source of my strength?

↪ Do I know how to comfort myself and be a friend to myself at all times, no matter what?

↪ What am I doing to establish and maintain loving relationships with the people closest to me?

↪ How well do I manage stress?

↪ Do I have good heath practices?

↪ Is my work satisfying?

↪ Am I satisfied with my spiritual path?

↪ What do I do to cultivate a sense of inner peace?

Appendix C
What Others Have to Say About the Akashic Records

When I first became aware of the meaning of the Akashic Records, I was profoundly touched. At that point I knew very little about my karmic evolution. I had pieces of information coming to me from different sources, but not any specific guidance as to how to properly access and utilized this ancient knowledge at will. I was full of questions; I was shy, introverted, [and] insecure, with an intellectually fabricated story of whom I had become. Added to that I was holding a rosary of excuses of why I have kept circling around those negative habitual patterns of behavior...over and over again. The Akashic Records transformed me as well as the way I started to relate to the outer world.

I took my first Intensive class with Ernesto, a wonderful and qualified teacher. And through such a gifted and genuinely sensitive instructor we received the Sacred Prayer; the crucial key to begin the divine dialogue with the Lords of Akasha or Karmic guardians. Ernesto patiently watched us take our first baby steps into this magnificent experience. He allowed us to discover the Records infinite qualities of love, clarity, wisdom, and transformative potential. And once there I felt myself immersed in pure Divine essence and bathed in blessings beyond language. I felt at home and welcomed.

Since then I have attended several Intensives and Akashic Records classes and the change has been inevitable. I have observed my transformation. Shyness became kindness, introversion became introspection, insecurity became confidence, and anger transformed into compassion and little by little my reactions evolved into careful actions.

To this day the Akashic Records continue to shape my spiritual landscape. They provide insightful advise, key instructions, divine guidance as well as trustful answers, when asked, including being able to write this testimonial.

Maria Romero
Miami, Florida

⌘

Though I was first introduced to the Akashic Records in the mid-70s through reading Edgar Cayce, it wasn't until I met Ernesto Ortiz that I really took the plunge into the very personal and immense *gift* that accessing one's Records is.

I took Level 1 and 2 from Ernesto when he came to Northern California in 2003. [I] experienced tears of great joy at the personal knowledge and healing that took place for me *and* simultaneously achieved clarity of purpose in wanting to join Ernesto's noble efforts in bringing the Akashic Records to humanity—establishing myself as a certified Akashic Records Consultant and then also becoming certified in 2004 to teach Level 1 classes and in 2007 to teach Level 2 classes.

Providing Akashic Records consultations and instruction to others has been incredibly satisfying for me as I've thereby assisted others as they heal, become empowered, and make wiser choices and create beneficial shifts in their lives. My greatest amount of gratitude, however, to Ernesto and to the Masters and Teachers, has been for the "wealth" I have received literally on a day-by-day basis from opening my own Records. Time and again, I have consulted my Records and received just what I needed to take the next best step in my life (even in cases where that step was to actually "do nothing" and allow other things to shift first!).

One of my most enjoyable and beneficial applications of this tool has been to consistently open my Records during my twice-daily yoga/meditation practice. Impossible, of course, to do a simultaneous "do it, not-do-it" comparison, yet I can state with much confidence that the depth of my meditations and the opening of my body to more vital energy, strength, and flexibility has been a quantum leap above what I would expect from simply maintaining a daily practice.

I also often open my Records when in creativity mode with songwriting, and the increase in the ease of creative flow and the overall confidence in knowing I am fully present and tapping into greater realms of musical possibility and expression beyond what my mind or even my normal level of creativity could access, is a source of great joy for me (and for those around me, too, who are happily blown away with what comes through!).

As the song goes, "these are a few of my favorite things" when it comes to the purposes and impacts of accessing my Masters and Teachers through the Akashic Records. I know it's actually just the tip of the iceberg for what I have thus far done in a few years of using this cherished gift, let alone all of the new openings and avenues of growth that will be revealed to me in the thousands of times I will tap into my Records in the years ahead. It is an honor to be on this path with Ernesto and with the ever-growing number of glowing-growing souls who have or will soon be joining us on this journey to the heart!

John Fargo
Emeryville, California
www.JonTheMuse.com

↜↝

From as long as I can remember I could always "see" things, sense or know things before they happened. It seemed like my life was in a constant déjà vu state.

As I [grew] older and there were additional stresses added to my life such as a family, mortgage, and so on, it appeared that I could no longer see as clearly or as vividly as I used to. What most people do not realize is that as our physical and energetic bodies become overtaxed, there seems to be a fog that comes with it. This fog affects our clarity. Then, to add to that, the speed at which our society has decided to live has become overwhelming. When we do not take the time to truly connect with ourselves and ask all of the questions and nuances about situations, relationships, and opportunities, we start to make assumptions. Those assumptions can cause us unnecessary grief and sorrow. From there we start to mistrust our guidance or give up on listening to our inner selves altogether because we believe it is never right. That is where I was many years ago.

So I ask you this, as I had to ask myself: How can you hear the words of love if you do not love yourself? The Akashic Records came to me at a time when I doubted my guidance, my intuition, me.

When I took the course and realized how simple, how beautiful, how loving it was, I was hooked for life. I was finally able to hear the guidance that I craved to heal relationships with others and with myself on a whole new level. I was able to go forward confidently after my dreams and goals in my career. I was better able to nurture and love my children and my husband. I am able to now take stock [of] what is truly important in my life and what can fall away so that every day becomes easier and easier.

It was through the Akashic Records that I chose to listen to them and open my wellness centre. With the help of the Masters and Teachers I was able to find a location, design the space, [and] bring forward amazing people to create my vision and participate as healers within. It became so easy that some days I have to pinch myself. One example of their beautiful knowledge is that I was told of eight wonderful individuals who would start with me and then leave quickly. This was for my personal lesson on contractual items and hiring policies. How fun to go back through my journals and three months previous see that [I had received] their exact first names—before I had even met them! Through this kind of guidance you realize that everything has a purpose. There was no sorrow, no anger, just gratefulness for the beautiful lesson that helps me to move forward in my business.

The changes in my family, my home, my health and spirituality are undeniable. My own personal growth and ability to see the world for all of its beauty and opportunity is right there in front of me like a ripe piece of fruit waiting to be savoured.

There is no fear in my life, only fascination and observation in all that surrounds me. If something is unclear or unknown all I have to do is ask and it is revealed with such love that I am now able to see life as the beautiful blessing that it truly is. If I could share one tool with everyone that would provide them with unlimited potential it would be this.

In Gratitude,
Tracy Blehm
Lasya Healing Centre, Inc.
Calgary, Alberta, Canada
www.lasyahealing.com

The ability to connect and receive guidance and information from the Masters and Teachers of Akasha has had a profound effect on my life. To be able to receive trusted high vibrational information from these sacred Teachers is a precious gift.

When I enter the Akashic Records I sense that my very strong analytical mind gets quiet and I connect with the wisdom of my heart and my inner voice.

Surprises often await me.

The Masters always guide me with positive thoughts. The most important one has been, life can be lived with ease. For many years my mind would convince me that I had more value as a person if I did things which were difficult and complicated. I am amazed how much I can accomplish with the belief that I can follow a path of ease and simplicity. This has been the most important teaching I have received and adopted. The Masters often teach using superb images and great humor; it feels like the laughing Buddha is telling me to lighten up.

When I am preparing to do vibrational healing work I call on the Masters and Teachers to protect and guide me. I feel more centered and trusting with the knowledge they are present and this allows me to channel vibrational sound and healing energy with greater ease and pleasure.

The message "you are much loved" is often sent with each connection I have with the Masters and Teachers. It is like having a loving family wanting the very best for me, present [for] and supportive [of] me on my path toward increased awareness and consciousness.

Namaste,
Elizabeth Wallace
Sutton, Québec City, Canada
www.elizabeth-wallace.com

⟜

My initiation into the Akashic Records by Ernesto has brought about a great deepening of awareness and a paradigm shift in my consciousness. Each time I connect with the Masters and Teachers, I come away with a deeper understanding of who I am, and what my tasks are this lifetime. There is also a sense of deep wisdom and trust; that the meaning of "greatest and highest" can be experienced in this sacred space. Many of the readings which I do for clients involve exploring the higher meaning of their life, what have they come to do. The answers which the Master and Teachers provide to these kinds of questions has led to a much expanded understanding of the true nature of one's karma. It is clear to me now that the greater structure of one's life is determined by one's higher self prior to birth. [It's] as if the soul went to the market and decided, *Let's see, I'll have a mother like this, a father like that, maybe a sibling or two. I want to be raised in a given culture and these are the tasks I want to achieve and or learnings that I want to experience.* For most individuals, the choices fade away in the course of the first few years of life, leaving the individual searching for a higher purpose to life....

The ability to ask for illumination from the Lords of the Akashic Records is a great blessing, allowing for those who seek it the possibility of clarifying the seeming mysteries of one's life. Often the answers which are provided require integration and the expansion of one's consciousness. Often it can be more painful to know the truth than if one had not asked, and this is one of the most powerful lessons for me. The choice to deepen one's search for truth can lead to a great deal of pain, but this pain can also be the path to greater healing and self-discovery. It is not a choice which should be taken lightly, yet the resulting growth and wisdom can take one to new levels of awareness.

In closing, my experiences with the Akashic Records have led me to a greater respect not only for myself and my clients, but all life everywhere. Everything has its place and purpose. We are all one.

V'asana Oannes
Zurich, Switzerland
www.dharmavibration.com

⯎

I am really honored to share my experience of the Akashic Records and its benefits. In 2007 I created my travel agency, and that same year I discovered the Akashic Records.

At the beginning when I first started to ask questions, I was surprised by some of the answers, but I followed the messages I received from the Lords of Akasha without questioning them.

I did not immediately understand why I was guided from point A to point Y and [only] then to point B, as a direct way would have seemed faster.

Then I understood with emotion that the Lords of Akasha, in their infinite grace, had guided me to places I had to experience and where I could learn how to grow, slowly and nicely, in order to be ready to carry on my mission on earth.

Little by little I created my travel agency specialized in spiritual travel, which has grown successfully since [its inception].

I feel immensely grateful for Ernesto, and for his extraordinary ability to teach this incredible tool with so much love and depth.

Love,
Eric Grange
Lyon, France
www.oasis-voyages.com

⯎

I am still amazed and...honored to have met the Akashic Records, this sacred dimension. This encounter has deeply changed my personal life and [my life] as a therapist.

My personal life: I can go further in the liberation of my old memories. It gives me a lot more strength. It helps me to develop again and again love inside of me toward myself and others. I feel more and more purified in my spiritual being.

As a therapist: It helps a lot the process of therapy, giving keys to people I accompany as well to free themselves from old chains within themselves and with their close relations, according to ancient karmic links, as well to develop in a clearer and more peaceful way that they have to realize in their lives, connected with their highest potentialities.

According to my feeling and experience, the Akashic Records are offered to us to help us to become [that which] we forgot: Light beings, connected with the Creator.

Bianca Saury
Therapist and Writer
Auch, France
www.lechantducoeur.org

⊖

I was asked how my life has changed and what healing has occurred for me personally by working with the Akashic Records. I smiled at this and thought back to when I was first introduced to this incredible work. ... [I]t all started when I arrived at the airport, the day before the Akashic Record intensive classes began, where I was refused admittance to fly into Canada from the states. It's a long story.

...I finally arrive the morning of class and by the afternoon I was so entranced that the trip quickly faded from memory. The seven-day experience of being daily in the Akashic Records energy probably rewired parts of my brain and certainly my energy systems, for I have never been the same since.

Opening and spending time in the Akashic Records which reside within Akasha allows us to reconnect with our divine being. Within that sacred energy and the guidance given by the Masters and Teachers we are gently and lovingly led to wholeness by being shown whatever blockages are in the way of making that connection back to source and higher self. In other words, anything that is causing us pain is brought to light and dissolved or shifted to allow for a healing to occur.

For me healing has and continues to occur in every aspect of my life, from curing self-esteem and debilitating social phobias to depression and an unbalanced and inaccurate self-image. Changing one thing changes everything. Life goals are changing, relationships blossoming or dissolving, creative expression takes on a whole new magic. I don't worry anymore—it's all good.

The old patterns have been unraveled. The memories don't trigger me and I actually feel like they happened to someone else. I don't care what is unknown or untried. It all just makes me giggle instead of sending me to my bed to cower under the covers or to the refrigerator for a quart of Ben and Jerry's ice cream. How awesome is that?

In writing this I suddenly realize that in all the self-improvement work I have done in my life—which was a lot, believe me—there was an intellectual, rational change which...led me to where I am now. The difference for me is that when I am in the Akashic Records and listening, really hearing and understanding what the Masters and Teachers are telling me, and applying it to my thoughts and life, there's a shift that happens starting at the soul level and growing up and through all the layers and divisions and compartments we have as a part of being human. It's like being immersed once again in the very waters of life, and it slowly cleanses away all of the darkness and dirt we have accumulated. I laugh—well, of course [I do]: I am getting guidance from ascended beings and reconnecting with my source.... Nothing else could happen.

When we can just for a moment, a brief moment in time, see ourselves as we truly are in the incredible complexity and eternal magnificence that we have forgotten, our soul sighs in relief, and this life we are living out is put finally into a new perspective. It's suddenly child's play.

Julie Katzer
Spokane, Washington
www.akashicrecordsconsultations.com

The connection with the Masters and Teachers of Akasha feels like coming home, to this place where precious insights, comfort, and unconditional love are waiting for me, always available as long as it is my pure, humble, and sincere heart's calling. Following the reconnection path of my soul under the powerful loving guidance of Ernesto has led me to reestablish the contact with Akasha on a daily basis.

Not only precious insights but also streams and showers of high frequency loving energies come down on me, day after day. Held in this embrace, I can suddenly see beyond the boundaries of my little self, heal, and grow.

The most amazing [thing] is how quick and immediate the benefits are. Old wounds can surface in this safe place, be seen, acknowledged, and healed. Currently, thanks to Ernesto's guidance into the world of Akasha, I learn more about life and feel more complete than ever before, since I could already welcome quite a few lost parts of my soul back inside of me.

Tina Hellingrath
Toulouse, France

Appendix D
About the Akashic Records Levels 2 and 3

The Akashic Records Levels 2 and 3 are offered by Ernesto Ortiz and other certified instructors under Journey to the Heart. Levels 2 and 3 are offered during a live class only. This is essential because of the dynamics created with the participants. In the Level 2 class there are *dyads*, interactions with one or more participants to formulate and answer questions. The Level 2 class can bring the student to the level of consultant if the person so desires.

In the Level 2 class students learn to open the Akashic Records for others. As in Level 1, they work with the art of translating the information received from our Masters and Teachers, and become attuned to the essence of pure love, light, and Spirit. This two-day class gives students the opportunity to deepen their personal healing and adds to the experience from Level 1 as they enter the sacred space of another seeker to access their Akashic Records. In many cases, this experience is life-transforming for the individual receiving the information.

The Level 2 class offers the opportunity to fine-tune students' reception of information, as they not only receive information but also share it through the power of the spoken word.

During this class students are able to work with fellow consultants as they team up and practice opening the Akashic Records for each other. They have the opportunity to have their Records read and, in the process, to validate their own answers. In working with others, students will be opening to receive the information in ways that they have not experienced before. They set themselves into the mode of pure and unconditional service to others and share the sounds, tastes, feelings, and emotions that they receive. It is often a time to invite loved ones to come in and communicate unfinished business, express love, or ask for forgiveness and resolution with the person for whom a student is reading.

Students in this class also learn the Level 2 Grace Points, how to deal with patterns of interference, how to formulate better questions, how to create a sacred space, and additional meditations to increase their own vibrational frequency.

The Akashic Records Level 3 class is an integration of the previous two classes and a deepening of the Akashic Records experience. This class is about *each student* and the deep personal healing that is possible once one gets below the surface and into the root system of the self. This system is what feeds us, what gives us nourishment, and it is active within the self 24 hours a day. It is part of the subconscious and unconscious programming , the robotic responses that we all carry within the self.

In Level 3 students learn how to identify *Imaginal cells* and what to do about them. They also tap into the energy of the Amos code, God's code or fingerprint within us, and awaken it to create a magnificent life. They also learn the advanced Grace Points, some of which will help to disarm the Imaginal cells and some that will help anchor the new Amos code and other positive experiences.

In the Level 3 class we explore:

- The art of questioning.
- How to formulate questions that can take you deeper.
- Ancestral healing patterns.
- Personal genealogy and how it is playing into your life.
- DNA and personal relationships.
- Advanced Grace Points.
- Imaginal cells and how they play a major role in your life.
- How to uncover and activate the Amos code, the code within the DNA as God's signature that contains the message of healing and peace.

- How to use the physical body to anchor all information and energy received.
- How to transform addictions and fears into friends and allies—powerful material that will help students conquer their inner demons.

Bibliography

Cameron, Julia. *The Artist's Way: A Spiritual Path to Higher Creativity*. New York: Jeremy P. Tarcher/Putnam, 1992.

Chia, Mantak. *Awaken Healing Light of the Tao*. Edited by Judith Stein. Chiang Mai, Thailand: Universal Tao Publications, 1993.

Haanel, Charles F. *The Amazing Secrets of the Yogi*. Wilder Publications, 2009.

Leadbeater, C. W. *The Chakras*. Wheaton, IL: Quest Books, 1973.

Ortiz, Ernesto. "2012 as the End of a Cosmic Cycle." *Scientific American* (September 1995).

"Paper 25: The Messenger Hosts of Space." *The Urantia Book: A Revelation*. Uversa Press, 2003.

Plotkin, Bill. *Nature and the Human Soul: Cultivating Wholeness and Community in a Fragmented World*. Novato, Calif.: New World Library, 2008.

Redmond, Layne, *Chakra Meditation*. Boulder, Colo.: Sounds True, Inc., 2004.

Rinpoche, Phakyab. *Phowa, The Profound Transference Path*. Class Manual, 2010.

Rinpoche, Sogyal. *The Tibetan Book of Living and Dying*. San Francisco, Calif.: Harper San Francisco, 1994.

"Special Issue: Crossroads for Planet Earth." *Scientific American* (September 2005).

"Spiritual Research Into the Causes and Treatment of Additions: A Spiritual Perspective." Spiritual Science Research Foundation: *www.spiritualresearchfoundation.org*.

Williamson, Marianne. "Vision." From *A Return to Love: Reflections on the Principles of a Course in Miracles*. New York: HarperCollins Publishers, Inc., 1992, p. 190.

Index

About the Author

Ernesto Ortiz is the founder and director of Journey to the Heart, a company dedicated to the uplifting of consciousness and the well-being of people. Ernesto is a rare and gifted man whose experiences and studies have encompassed a broad scope of knowledge. He is a noted artist and author, a renowned and inspiring facilitator, teacher, and therapist recognized for his innovative, explorative, and multidimensional training.

Ernesto has devoted his life to exploring and communicating the language of the heart, primal movement, and deep inner spaces. During the past 25 years, Ernesto has taken thousands of people on a journey from physical and emotional inertia to the freedom of ecstasy, from the chaos of the chattering ego-mind to the blessed emptiness of stillness and inner silence. His workshops and retreats have an electric intensity that unifies the spiritual with the mundane, and includes everything from the poetic discovery of the soul to the modern approach of ancient shamanic practices. He has facilitated hundreds of workshops and seminars in the United States, Canada, France, Australia, the Caribbean, Indonesia, Egypt, the UK, Mexico, and South America. Ernesto breathes new life into his audiences with his enlightening perspectives, humorous stories, and practical action steps. His words of wisdom inspire minds, open hearts, and motivate people to action. His understanding of the power of unconditional love and acceptance is what provides the room for personal transformation. His methodologies and teachings are transforming the lives of hundreds of thousands of people around the world.

Ernesto's deep and intimate connection with the Akashic Records began in 1993, after being deeply touched by the material. Upon seeing his life transformed, he began assisting in numerous Akashic Records classes and, with the guidance from the Masters, started teaching in 1997.

Ernesto has two amazing children and makes his home base in Miami, Florida.

↔

For Akashic Records classes and intensives as well as certified consultants under Journey to the Heart, visit our Website: *www.journeytotheheart.com*.

For free meditations, music, and more visit: *www.journeytotheheart.com* and click **Free Stuff**.

For custom-made smudging fans, visit: *www.journeytotheheart.com*.

If you want a more directed approach to the material and wish to receive a direct transmission, you can attend a live class where the energy of the group directs the flow of the class and you have direct contact with a teacher. As an alternative, you can also purchase the Level I class on four DVDs from *www.journeytotheheart.com*.

Also by Ernesto Ortiz

Hot Stone Massage

In the Presence of Love

The Akashic Records Level I (Set of four DVDs)

Tian Di Bamboo Massage (DVD)